T0365322

Cambridge Elements ☰

Elements in Econophysics
edited by
Rosario Nunzio Mantegna
University of Palermo
Bikas K. Chakrabarti
Saha Institute of Nuclear Physics
Mauro Gallegati
Polytechnic University of Marche, Ancona
Irena Vodenska
Boston University

THE κ-STATISTICS APPROACH TO INCOME DISTRIBUTION ANALYSIS

Fabio Clementi
University of Macerata

Mauro Gallegati
Polytechnic University of Marche, Ancona

Lisa Gianmoena
University of Pisa

Giorgio Kaniadakis
Polytechnic University of Turin

Simone Landini
IRES Piemonte, Torino

CAMBRIDGE
UNIVERSITY PRESS

CAMBRIDGE
UNIVERSITY PRESS

Shaftesbury Road, Cambridge CB2 8EA, United Kingdom

One Liberty Plaza, 20th Floor, New York, NY 10006, USA

477 Williamstown Road, Port Melbourne, VIC 3207, Australia

314–321, 3rd Floor, Plot 3, Splendor Forum, Jasola District Centre,
New Delhi – 110025, India

103 Penang Road, #05–06/07, Visioncrest Commercial, Singapore 238467

Cambridge University Press is part of Cambridge University Press & Assessment,
a department of the University of Cambridge.

We share the University's mission to contribute to society through the pursuit of
education, learning and research at the highest international levels of excellence.

www.cambridge.org
Information on this title: www.cambridge.org/9781009446358
DOI: 10.1017/9781009446341

When citing this work, please include a reference to the DOI 10.1017/9781009446341

First published 2025

A catalogue record for this publication is available from the British Library

ISBN 978-1-009-44635-8 Paperback
ISSN 2754-6071 (online)
ISSN 2754-6063 (print)

Additional resources for this publication at www.cambridge.org/clementi

The κ-Statistics Approach to Income Distribution Analysis

Elements in Econophysics

DOI: 10.1017/9781009446341
First published online: April 2025

Fabio Clementi
University of Macerata

Mauro Gallegati
Polytechnic University of Marche, Ancona

Lisa Gianmoena
University of Pisa

Giorgio Kaniadakis
Polytechnic University of Turin

Simone Landini
IRES Piemonte, Torino

Author for correspondence: Fabio Clementi, fabio.clementi@unimc.it

Abstract: This Element presents the κ-generalized distribution, a statistical model tailored for the analysis of income distribution. Developed over years of collaborative, multidisciplinary research, it clarifies the statistical properties of the model, assesses its empirical validity, and compares its effectiveness with other parametric models. It also presents formulas for calculating inequality indices within the κ-generalized framework, including the widely used Gini coefficient and the relatively lesser-known Zanardi index of Lorenz curve asymmetry. Through empirical illustrations, the book criticizes the conventional application of the Gini index, pointing out its inadequacy in capturing the full spectrum of inequality characteristics. Instead, it advocates the adoption of the Zanardi index, accentuating its ability to capture the inherent heterogeneity and asymmetry in income distributions.

Keywords: income distribution, inequality, Gini coefficient, Zanardi index, κ-generalized distribution

JEL classifications: B59, C46, D31, D63

ISBNs: 9781009446358 (PB), 9781009446341 (OC)
ISSNs: 2754-6071 (online), 2754-6063 (print)

Contents

1 Introduction

The issue of income and wealth inequality has long been a focal point in economic literature, drawing contributions from numerous esteemed scholars. In the early stages of economic inquiry, when the discipline focused mainly on resource allocation and societal welfare, theoretical and methodological tools were comparatively rudimentary, and data availability was limited. As a result, classical economists concentrated on the "functional distribution" of income, analyzing its allocation among wages, profits, and rents. In contrast, contemporary economists place greater emphasis on the "personal distribution" of income, which looks at how income is distributed among individuals, irrespective of their role in production.

David Ricardo's "Principles" extensively explored the underlying laws governing income distribution. With the emergence of the marginalist and neoclassical revolutions, economic focus shifted towards the general equilibrium theory (GET), a framework still relevant today under the guise of DSGE (dynamic stochastic general equilibrium) methodology. However, this approach, rooted in the "representative agent" paradigm, tends to overlook income distribution dynamics. While income distribution and inequality have never been entirely sidelined, they have often taken a backseat to the pursuit of proving market equilibrium's existence, uniqueness, and stability under idealized assumptions.

Notably, applied mathematicians and statisticians, many hailing from Italy, have shown significant interest in the realm of income distribution and inequality. Figures such as Max Otto Lorenz, Vilfredo Pareto, Gaetano Pietra, Umberto Ricci, Corrado Gini, and Giampaolo Zanardi have made substantial contributions to this field, highlighting the interdisciplinary nature of the study of economic disparities. These scholars, among others, will be acknowledged in this Element.

Various definitions exist for income or wealth inequality, yet they converge on the idea that unequal distribution signifies uneven access to opportunities among individuals. The root causes of this disparity can vary widely, spanning global, local, and individual factors.

In many countries, there is a growing acknowledgment of widening gaps in income and wealth distribution, indicating a concerning trend towards heightened inequality. This consensus is underscored by various studies and reports, highlighting the significance of this issue within both academic circles and among policymakers.

The issue of inequality in the distribution of income and wealth has recently taken center stage in political debates, sparking renewed interest among scholars. Key contributions to this discussion include works by Atkinson (2015), Atkinson & Piketty (2007), Piketty (2014), and Stiglitz (2012, 2015).

For policymakers in particular, it is imperative to develop theories and models rooted in robust empirical evidence. Thus, there is a need to utilize precise methodologies to determine the most accurate parametric distributions of income and wealth, as well as to identify the most reliable estimators for measuring inequality.

Inequality is a phenomenon that fluctuates across time and space, with a persistent presence throughout history and likely into the future. It stems from various factors, including the behaviors of individuals holding a transferable quantity like income or wealth, as well as broader environmental conditions such as political, cultural, and economic contexts. The uneven distribution of these resources underscores the disparity in opportunities among individuals.

Some contend that inequality is an inevitable outcome, while others see it as fulfilling a social function by incentivizing advancement and progress. However, the crux of the matter lies in the detrimental effects of inequality, as it perpetuates cycles of poverty and deprivation. While complete eradication may prove elusive, effective control through redistributive or protective policies is essential. These policies should prioritize crucial aspects such as ensuring access to quality healthcare and education, particularly for disadvantaged groups, as these are vital for unlocking better job prospects and opportunities.

The management of inequality is critical for its mitigation. Achieving this goal necessitates the development and application of robust theoretical and methodological frameworks to comprehend and gauge its extent accurately.

For example, while economic growth is typically seen as positive news, its benefits are not always evenly distributed among individuals. In some rapidly growing economies, we have observed an exacerbation of inequality, as only a select few reap substantial rewards, particularly when considering both the financial and real sectors of the economy. Therefore, true economic growth should extend its benefits to all members of society, ideally favoring those who are most disadvantaged. Sustainable growth is characterized by a balanced distribution of wealth, steering clear of extreme social stratification and ensuring a high quality of life for the majority, if not all, citizens. However, achieving this requires a thorough understanding of inequality, underpinned by robust theoretical frameworks and analytical tools that can accurately measure its extent within the mechanisms of economies.

Over the years, numerous theoretical models and inequality estimators have been proposed and explored, making it impractical to list or review them all here. Each proposal has its strengths and weaknesses, contributing to the ongoing discourse without yielding a definitive solution. In this context, this Element presents the most effective and up-to-date solutions available for inferring both the parametric distribution of income and wealth, as well as the appropriate measures of inequality. Specifically, it introduces the κ-generalized distribution and the Zanardi index of asymmetry as prominent tools in this endeavor. These approaches offer valuable insights into understanding and addressing the complexities of economic inequality in contemporary society.

A quantity is deemed "positive" if all its values are nonnegative. Furthermore, a positive quantity is considered "transferable" if a portion held by one observation unit can be transferred to another without altering the total available quantity through interaction. This transferable quantity is termed "diffused" when the ensemble of N units possesses nonuniform shares of the total amount. Conversely, if each unit holds an identical share of $1/N$, the quantity is deemed "equi-distributed" among individuals.

When the distribution disproportionately favors certain individuals or groups, it is categorized as "concentrated." Thus, while all transferable quantities are inherently diffused, the degree and shape of the distribution can vary widely, ranging from equi-distribution with minimal concentration to maximum concentration, where one unit possesses nearly the entire quantity while the remaining $N - 1$ units possess negligible amounts.

We can unambiguously refer to equi-distribution when each individual holds an equal fraction, representing the scenario with minimal concentration. However, the opposite extreme, characterized by maximum concentration, lacks a specific term. In essence, between these theoretical extremes, lies a spectrum of situations with varying degrees of concentration. While the term equi-distribution implies equality, other distribution scenarios inherently involve some degree of inequality. Although this terminology is intuitive, it may not capture the nuanced variations effectively.

Equality can be conceptualized as a state of distribution devoid of any disparities. Conversely, when a transfer mechanism operates within a heterogeneous population, interacting through a complex network of relationships, inequality emerges.[1] This inequality can either intensify over time as distributive imbalances exacerbate or diminish as such imbalances ease. Unlike the idealized state of equality, which represents homogeneity, inequality is a persistent condition characterized by varying degrees of heterogeneity.

The κ-generalized distribution, initially proposed by Kaniadakis (2001) in the field of nonlinear particle physics kinetics and further refined over the

---

[1] For instance, refer to the zero-intelligence agents model by Yakovenko and Rosser (2009).

following two decades, has recently found application in economics, thanks to studies by, among others, Clementi, Di Matteo, Gallegati, and Kaniadakis (2008), Clementi and Gallegati (2016), and Clementi, Gallegati, and Kaniadakis (2007, 2009, 2010, 2012a, 2012b). These works demonstrate that this distribution offers a superior fit compared to well-known functional forms such as the Singh–Maddala, Dagum type I, and GB2 models.

The asymmetry index of the Lorenz curve, introduced by Zanardi (1964, 1965), employs a geometric decomposition method popularized by Tarsitano (1987, 1988). Recent research by Clementi, Gallegati, Gianmoena, Landini, and Stiglitz (2019) and Gallegati, Landini, and Stiglitz (2016) has shown that this index outperforms the traditional Gini concentration index in measuring inequality.

Both the κ-generalized distribution and the Zanardi index serve as essential analytical and theoretical tools for understanding and quantifying income and wealth distribution inequality. They are invaluable for academic research as well as applied studies aimed at informing policy-making efforts.

This Element is structured as follows.

In Section 2, we provide a brief overview of existing methods for analyzing income distribution, focusing primarily on the Lorenz curve and traditional inequality measures. We then introduce novel insights into inequality measurement by addressing the asymmetry inherent in this curve. Specifically, we introduce the Zanardi index of asymmetry as a superior measure of inequality. Unlike other measures, this index considers both the intensity and direction of inequality within the distribution, facilitating comparisons even when Lorenz curves intersect. Empirical space-time estimates and comparisons with other indices, notably the Gini index, which only addresses concentration, support the superiority of the Zanardi index.

Section 3 presents the κ-generalized distribution, offering comprehensive mathematical details regarding its origin, limit cases, definitions, and fundamental properties. It explores the parametric specification of the Lorenz curve and various indices associated with this distribution. Additionally, the methodology for parameter estimation is elucidated, along with insights gleaned from applying this model to real income distribution data.

Section 4 provides many up-to-date applications of the κ-generalized distribution to real-world income data, showing fitting results and comparing them with those obtained from other parametric models.

Section 5 concludes this Element with essential reflections. While acknowledging that no result can be deemed definitively absolute, akin to physics, some findings can be deemed sufficiently robust until proven otherwise, especially if they offer superior explanations for known phenomena. This Element aspires to contribute to such advancements, and we invite readers to engage in further improving the results presented herein.

2 New Insights on the Measurement of Inequality

2.1 The Inequality Measures

The growing attention to economic inequality has revived debates on the most suitable metric or index for measuring income inequality. Since the introduction of the Lorenz curve in 1905, which shows the share of income or wealth accruing to the bottom x percent of the population, numerous indices have been proposed to assess economic inequality.

The Gini (1914) coefficient stands as the predominant and extensively employed measure of income inequality. This metric measures inequality by calculating the area between the Lorenz curve, representing income distribution, and the line of perfect equality.

Based on the Lorenz curve, the literature on inequality has introduced alternative metrics, including the Pietra–Ricci index (Pietra, 1915; Ricci, 1916) and the Zanardi index (Zanardi, 1964, 1965), which provide new insights into income inequality. The Pietra–Ricci focuses on the redistribution needed to achieve equality, while the Zanardi index explores the asymmetry on the income distribution.[2]

Other indices, like the Theil index, are grounded in information theory (Shorrocks, 1980; Theil, 1967), while some, like the Atkinson (1970) index, are welfare-based measures of inequality and are more responsive to value judgments regarding inequality aversion. Though these indices offer valuable insights into the complex nature of inequality, each comes with its strengths and limitations. The choice of an index depends on the specific aspect of inequality under consideration and the societal values deemed most important.

In particular, indices that satisfy the three axiomatic conditions of (i) symmetry, (ii) scale invariance, and the (iii) transfer principle produce identical rankings for distinct income distributions only if the Lorenz curves do not intersect.[3] Likewise, rankings based on the Atkinson index remain consistent regardless of the level of risk aversion, only if the Lorenz curves do not

---

[2] The Pietra–Ricci index represents the proportion of income needed for redistribution to achieve perfect equality, visually represented as the maximum vertical distance between the Lorenz curve and the 45-degree line. The index ranges from 0 to 1, where 0 represents perfect equality (all incomes are the same) and 1 represents perfect inequality (one person earns all the income).

[3] "Symmetry" requires that, as income levels among individuals change, a society's assessment of inequality remains unchanged. "Scale invariance" requires the inequality index to be invariant to equi-proportional changes of the original incomes. Finally, the "transfer principle" requires the inequality measure to change when income transfers occur among individuals in

intersect. If the Lorenz curves intersect, then different indices can yield different results depending on the type of inequality to which each index is most sensitive.

With the aim of discerning the nature of inequality, the Zanardi index distinguishes itself from the aforementioned indices by its capability to gauge the asymmetry of Lorenz curves. Unlike the previous measures, the Zanardi index delves into the shape of the distribution, aiding in the identification of whether inequality predominantly stems from the conditions of the poor or from the concentration of wealth among the richest.

2.2 Exploring the Lorenz Curve and the Gini Index Logic

It is well known that the most popular tool used to represent income distribution is the Lorenz curve $L(p)$, whose upward and convex trend is strongly affected by how income is concentrated/distributed among individuals. The $L(p)$, whose formalization is discussed in Section 3.2.2, tells us which proportion of the total income is in the hands of a given percentage of population. If income is distributed homogeneously among individuals, the Lorenz curve coincides with the main diagonal of a unit square, showing an absence of income concentration.

However, real-world income distribution is characterized by disparities between poor and rich people. This implies that less affluent individuals hold a share of total income below an equi-distributed allocation, while wealthier individuals hold more. Consequently, for typical income distributions, the Lorenz curve deviates from the diagonal, assuming the shape of a convex curve.

Closely tied to the representation of the Lorenz curve $L(p)$, the Italian statistician Corrado Gini, in 1914, introduced a synthetic measure known as the Gini coefficient. This coefficient quantifies the ratio of the area between the Lorenz Curve and the equi-distribution line (hereinafter referred to as the concentration area) to the area of maximum concentration. It is crucial to emphasize that the Gini index specifically conveys information about the concentration of transferable quantities. However, it falls short in capturing other critical dimensions of inequality, such as the extent of *heterogeneity*, *concentration*, and *asymmetry* inherent in income distribution (Clementi et al., 2019; Gallegati et al., 2016).

The concept of *heterogeneity* underscores the presence of a nonuniform distribution of economic resources among different socioeconomic groups (poor

---

the income distribution – in particular, inequality indices should fall with a progressive transfer, that is, an income transfer from richer to poorer individuals, and rise with a regressive transfer, that is, an income transfer from poorer to richer individuals.

and rich), with implications for understanding the dynamics of income inequality within a society; the *concentration* means considering different degrees of disparity between the classes, while the concept of *asymmetry* refers to the directional disparity in the distribution of endowments.

In particular, asymmetry implies that the distribution reveals a certain direction of the income imbalance which could be "right-wards" if the rich class of the distribution is more heterogeneous than the poor one, or "left-wards" in the opposite scenario.[4] These three concepts – concentration, heterogeneity, and asymmetry – are crucial for a thorough understanding of inequality. Consequently, it is necessary to consider alternative measures that can examine for the shape of Lorenz curves.

2.3 The Zanardi Asymmetry Index of the Lorenz Curve

In what follows, we provide a description and an interpretation of the Zanardi (1964, 1965) index, which can be considered as a superior measure for examining income inequality, particularly in the presence of asymmetric income distributions. As highlighted by Clementi et al. (2019), Gallegati et al. (2016) and Park, Kim, and Ju (2021) inequality is characterized not only by its "intensity" but also by its "direction." In this framework, the "direction" of the inequality is discussed in terms of a positive and transferable quantity, such as income, which is unevenly distributed among recipients. This uneven distribution implies a form of "right-wing" or "left-wing" inequality concentration, highlighting the asymmetry of the Lorenz curve $L(p)$.

Graphically, this situation is illustrated in Figure 2.1(a). Consider two intersecting Lorenz curves: one with a "bulge" in the lower-income segment (solid line) and the other with a "bulge" in the wealthier segment (dashed line); in this case, even though the areas enclosed by the two Lorenz curves and the diagonal of the unit square are the same, the income share (qth) of the poorest fraction (pth) of the population is lower in the first distribution than in the second, although the income concentration is exactly equal.

Figure 2.1(a) shows two contrasting scenarios: one where the rich are very rich and get a high share of the total income, represented by the dashed curve, and another where the poor are very poor and get a very small share of the income, depicted by the solid curve.

In this framework, the discussion of the asymmetry of the $L(p)$ will be in terms of the discriminant point $D(p_d, q_d)$, which separates the poor class from

---

[4] If a rightward asymmetry of the Lorenz curve is detected, it indicates that the concentration on the rich side of the distribution is greater than that on the poor side. Conversely, if we observe a leftward asymmetry, it indicates a greater concentration on the poor side.

Econophysics

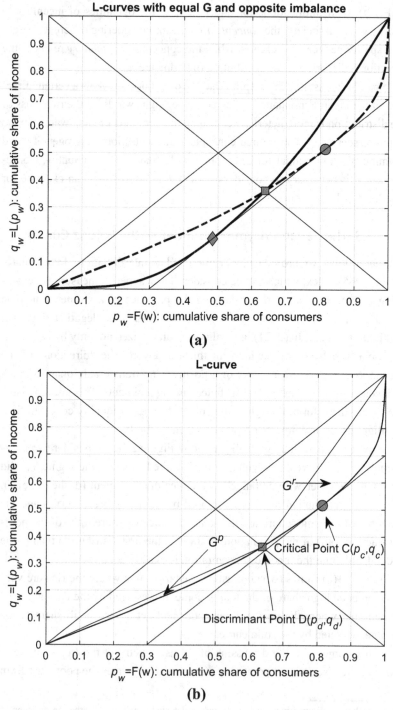

Figure 2.1 Two Lorenz curves with the same Gini index and opposite asymmetry (a); the characteristic point, discriminant point, and critical point of the Lorenz curve (b)

Note: See also Clementi et al. (2019).

the rich one, given by the intersection of the Lorenz curve with the negative bisector $q = 1 - p$, that is, the "axis of symmetry." Thus, the share of poor income earners within the population is given by p_d and accumulates a share q_d of total income, which is larger than the income share $(1 - q_d)$ accumulated by the $(1 - p_d)$ rich. The discriminant point $D(p_d, q_d)$ plays a relevant role, since it separates the total area under the Lorenz curve in two sub-areas from which the Gini indexes for the poor and the rich (G^p and G^r, respectively) can be estimated (see Figure 2.1(b)).

Based on the discriminant point $D(p_d, q_d)$, the Zanardi (1964, 1965) index can be defined as

$$Z = 2K\frac{\delta}{G}, \tag{2.1}$$

where $K = \frac{p_d q_d}{2}$, $\delta = G^r - G^p$ denotes the disparity of concentration between the rich and poor, and G is the overall Gini ratio. The index varies between -1 and 1, where $Z < 0$ means that the Lorenz curve is negatively asymmetric (or asymmetric to the left), while for $Z > 0$ the curve is positively asymmetric (or asymmetric to the right).

Therefore, if $G^r > G^p$ then $Z > 0$: the poor side is less concentrated than the rich one, or similarly the rich are more heterogeneous and concentrated than the poor, hence the distribution disadvantages the poor as they are more within-homogeneously poor than the rich side. In this case we face distributional imbalance toward the top (top-inequality), as described by the dashed curve in Figure 2.1(a). If $G^r < G^p$ then $Z < 0$ and the opposite interpretation holds: the poor exhibit greater heterogeneity and concentration compared to the rich, suggesting an imbalance distribution toward the bottom (bottom-inequality) – in other words, there are more ways of being poor than rich. This corresponds to the solid curve in Figure 2.1(a). Obviously, $Z = 0$ if the Lorenz curve is symmetric and no distributional imbalances are found, therefore inequality can be analyzed looking at the overall Gini index.

In this scenario, the Zanardi index may provide more insightful information than the Gini index, especially for distributions that exhibit the same G (i.e. the same level of concentration of $L(p)$) but differ in the sign of Z (i.e. $Z > 0$, indicating "right-wing" skewness of $L(p)$, or $Z < 0$, indicating "left-wing" skewness of $L(p)$).

2.4 Empirical Insights on Inequality

This section briefly presents some empirical evidence on inequality measures estimated using the Luxembourg Income Study (LIS) Database. The LIS Database provides public access to granular household-level income data for 52 countries, including both developed and developing nations over a period spanning 1963 to 2022.[5] Using a harmonized and equivalized dataset,[6] we explore the dynamics of disposable household income across 822 distributions.[7]

Figure 2.2 shows the relationship between the concentration index G and the entropy inequality indexes: mean logarithmic deviation (MLD), Theil, and Atkinson (with inequality aversion parameter equal to 1).[8] Although each index provides a distinct viewpoint on inequality, it is possible to observe that higher levels of concentration are associated with higher levels of distributive imbalances. For lower levels of concentration, all the indices are almost equivalent in classifying distributions, but for higher levels of concentration, the indices diverge while maintaining the same order. This pattern confirms a strong relationship between concentration and inequality, however, it does not offer insights into the specific nature or direction of the inequality.

Figure 2.3 illustrates the relationship between the general concentration index G and the concentration levels on the rich (G^r) and poor (G^p) side. The graph unveils a distributional imbalance stemming from varying concentration levels between the two segments of the distribution – that is, the rich and poor segments – indicating a directional aspect of inequality not fully captured by the Gini index. Furthermore, it appears that the Gini index makes little distinction between sampling from the rich or the poor sides of the distribution. The estimates provided in Figure 2.3 show that a 1% increase in concentration on

---

[5] To preserve confidentiality, access to microdata is conducted remotely, meaning that the program code is sent to LIS rather than being run directly by the user on the data. All code for processing LIS data has been developed using R, the open-source statistical software by R Core Team (2024), and is made available as supplementary material accompanying this Element.

[6] The LIS equivalence scale (square root of the number of household members) has been used. Before equivalization, top and bottom coding is applied by setting boundaries for extreme values of log-transformed disposable household income at the 75th percentile ($Q3$) plus 3 times the interquartile range ($Q3 - Q1$), and at the 25th percentile ($Q1$) minus 3 times the interquartile range. To ensure representativeness, our methodology employs person-level adjusted weights.

[7] The country datasets that are publicly accessible can be found listed on the LIS website at the following URL: www.lisdatacenter.org/our-data/lis-database/. The results presented in this section are the outcome of analyses conducted prior to the update of the LIS Database in March 2024, which included an additional number of datasets into the database. The subsequent Section 4 will refer to this updated version of the LIS Database for the results of the analyses presented therein.

[8] Each index offers a different perspective on inequality, with varying sensitivities to different parts of the income distribution and different societal preferences regarding inequality aversion. The MLD gives more weight to deviations of incomes at the lower end of the distribution, making it sensitive to changes in the bottom part of the income distribution. The Theil index is often used in socioeconomic contexts to understand both overall inequality and how it is distributed across different subgroups, while the Atkinson index penalizes high incomes more heavily than other measures like the Gini coefficient, making it sensitive to changes in the top end of the income distribution.

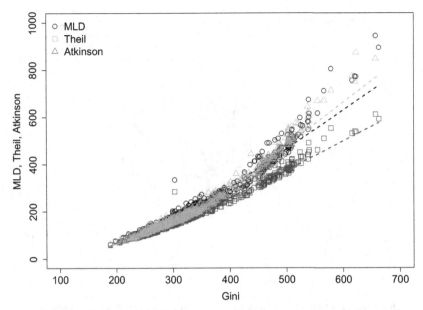

Figure 2.2 Relationship between concentration and entropy indexes of inequality ($\times 1,000$)

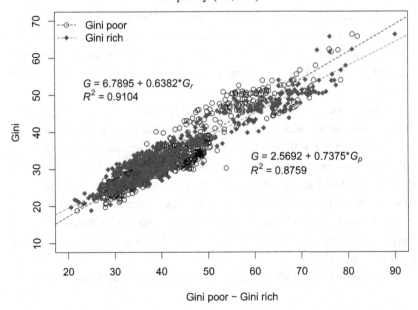

Figure 2.3 Overall Gini index, G, together with the concentration on the rich, G^r, and the poor, G^p, sides ($\times 100$)

the rich side increases the overall concentration by approximately 0.64%, while a similar increase on the poor side results in an approximately 0.74% boost in overall concentration. This preliminary analysis underscores that inequity is slightly driven by a higher concentration on the poor side rather than the

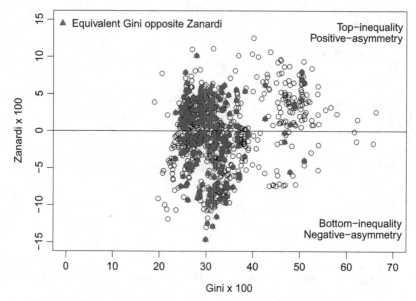

Figure 2.4 Overall Gini index, G, together with the Zanardi index, Z

rich side. The presence of such asymmetry enables a deeper understanding of the inequality directionality, particularly in this scenario where it is driven by the disadvantaged group. Consequently, exploring the concentration gap between the rich and the poor through the Zanardi index could offer valuable insights.

For this purpose, Figure 2.4 shows the Gini concentration index (horizontal axis) and the Zanardi asymmetry index (vertical axis), both estimated on the Lorenz curves for all distributions. Gray-triangular values denote cases of equivalent Gini paired with opposite Zanardi, indicating distributions with similar concentration but opposite asymmetry. For such observations, an analysis based solely on the Gini index would be misleading because, behind the same concentration value, different forms of inequality may be hidden, that is, top-inequality cases (above the horizontal axis) and bottom-inequality cases (below the horizontal axis).

At this point in the analysis, we can draw some preliminary conclusions:

1. The income distributions for the entire sample turn out to be very heterogeneous in terms of income concentration (Gini values ranging from a maximum of 0.6626 to a minimum of 0.1887).
2. Such distributions exhibit significant inequality or asymmetry in both the rich and poor segments, as described by the Zanardi index (with values ranging from a maximum of 0.1253 to a minimum of −0.1932).

In order to eliminate these distributional gaps, wealth transfers should be implemented to nullify both concentration ($G = 0$) and inequality ($Z = 0$). The Pietra–Ricci index (H) takes this aspect into account.

With reference to Figure 2.1(b), the Pietra–Ricci index measures the maximum distance of the Lorenz curve $q = L(p)$ from the equi-concentration segment, that is, the vertical distance of the critical point from the line of perfect equality. Starting with an income distribution characterized by $G > 0$ and $Z \neq 0$, it is possible to calculate the amount of income to transfer from a group (whether rich or poor) to achieve a distribution in which $G = 0$ and $Z = 0$, indicating the absence of inequality. As shown in Figure 2.5(a), as concentration levels increase, it will be necessary to transfer larger amounts of income to eliminate inequality. Thus, with reference to Figure 2.5(b), for values of $Z < 0$, it will be necessary to transfer a portion H of the total income from the poor class to the rich class to completely eliminate concentration and inequality – akin to a "Matthew" effect. In the case of $Z > 0$, on the other hand, the opposite will be necessary: transferring a portion of the total income from the rich class to the poor class – a kind of "Robin Hood" effect.

2.4.1 Examining the Inequality over Time

The analysis of inequality presented so far, while informative, is quite general and does not fully allow for an understanding of the time evolution of inequality. Furthermore, a misleading understanding of the concept of inequality becomes evident when solely focusing on the overall Gini index. A country-specific analysis provides a deeper understanding of the various forms of inequality within an economy, highlighting trends and potential divergences between the Gini and Zanardi indices.

With this purpose, Figures 2.6–2.9 show the time series of the Gini and Zanardi indices for a subset of countries with the highest number of consecutive years of data within the time period from 1990 to 2021. For the sake of exposition, we classify these economies into four groups: Anglo-Saxon countries (Canada, the United Kingdom, and the United States); Western European countries (France and Germany); Southern European countries (Italy and Spain); and Northern European countries (Denmark, Norway, and Sweden).

The United States (Figure 2.6(a)) shows an almost constant increase in the G concentration index throughout the period considered, with the exception of the last few years, where there is a marked decrease in the G index from values close to 0.39 to values close to 0.37. However, concerning the type of the inequality, there is a cyclical fluctuation between negative values of the Z index and values close to zero for almost the entire period. This increased inequality on the poor side, as indicated by negative Z values, is attributed to greater

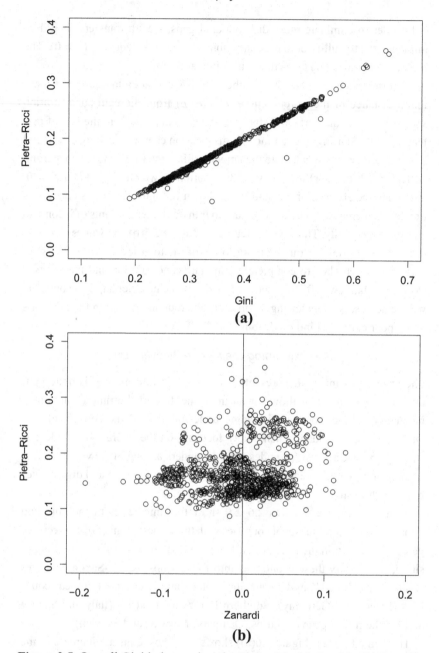

Figure 2.5 Overall Gini index against the Pietra–Ricci index (a); the Zanardi index against the Pietra–Ricci (b)

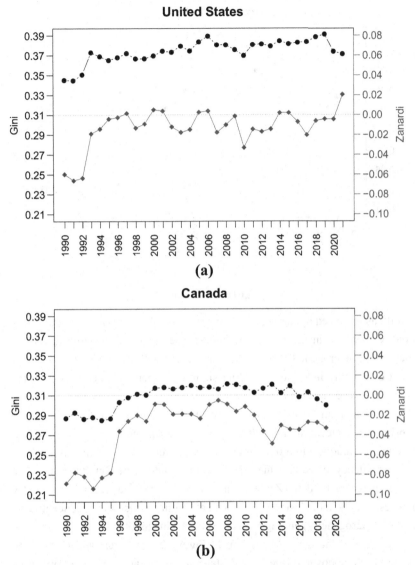

Figure 2.6 Temporal evolution of the Gini (bullets, left scale) and Zanardi (squares, right scale), Anglo-Saxon countries

Note: The horizontal line represents the zero reference line for the Zanardi index.

heterogeneity within the lower-income group, where individuals experience higher levels of poverty. These disparities on the side of the poor are mitigated in three time periods: 2000–2001, 2005–2006, and 2014–2015, during which the Zanardi index approaches zero, indicating a reduction in income distribution asymmetry, albeit with persistently high-income concentration values as indicated by the Gini index. In 2020–2021, however, the distribution undergoes

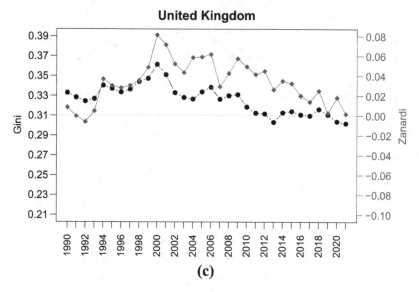

(c)

Figure 2.6 (Cont.)

a shift, as indicated by the positive Z values associated with an increase of inequality, this time in favor of the rich-side. The income distribution shows an increase in heterogeneity within the richer class, with the emergence of a segment of wealthy individuals holding significant shares of income within the richer class (i.e. the super-rich).

A similar trend, albeit with lower values, is observed for Canada (Figure 2.6(b)). The concentration levels of G increase throughout the first decade, stabilizing at values around 0.32 in the following ten years, and then fluctuating with a tendency to decrease in the last period. Although the Gini index shows an almost constant trend, the Z index values move further away from the symmetry line, especially in the last ten years, with a significant increase in concentration (hence heterogeneity) among the poor (bottom-inequality).

The case of the United Kingdom in Figure 2.6(c) differs and is, in some respects, the opposite of the United States and Canada, showing a downward trend in both the G and Z indices. The Zanardi index shows how, in the United Kingdom, the distributive imbalance has always favored the richer, with a tendency towards values close to zero only in recent years. We are therefore seeing a general reduction in concentration and inequality, particularly within the wealthy class, indicating a shift from a top-inequality profile to a bottom-inequality one.

Countries in Western Europe, like France and Germany, generally have lower levels of income concentration (Figure 2.7). France's Gini index shows a relatively stable trend over time, while Germany's Gini index depicts a rising trend. Both countries exhibit positive imbalances in income distribution, as

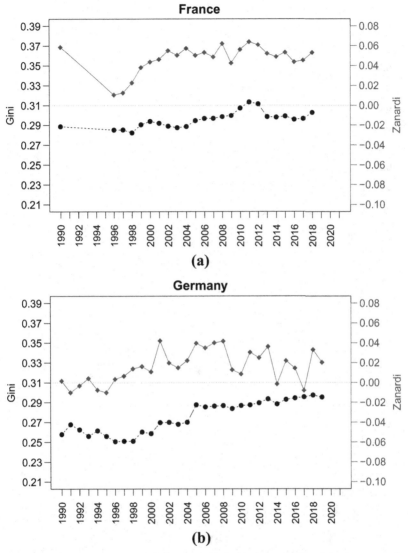

Figure 2.7 Temporal evolution of the Gini (bullets, left scale) and Zanardi (squares, right scale), Western European countries

Note: The horizontal line represents the zero reference line for the Zanardi index.

reflected by consistently positive values of *Z*. Consequently, a significant portion of total income in these economies is unequally distributed, with a larger proportion going to the rich while a smaller proportion is shared among the poor.

The situation in Southern European countries, specifically Italy and Spain, presents another interesting pattern (Figure 2.8). The Gini index shows relatively stable values over the years, around 0.33–0.35 for both countries.

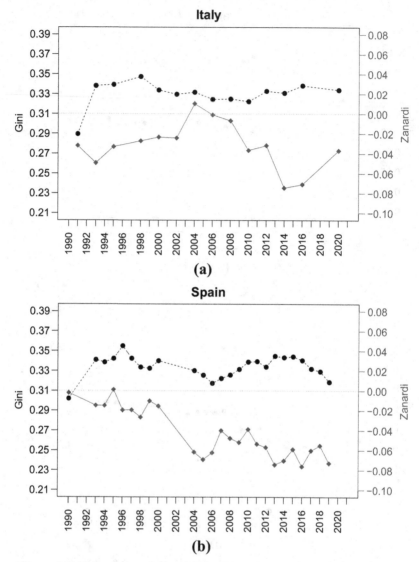

Figure 2.8 Temporal evolution of the Gini (bullets, left scale) and Zanardi
(squares, right scale), Southern European countries

Note: The horizontal line represents the zero reference line for the Zanardi index.

Conversely, the Zanardi index consistently falls below the symmetry line for
both economies, indicating strongly negative Z values. The two countries
have seen a notable rise in bottom-inequality, leading to increased poverty
among individuals. While the trend in Spain does not seem to be improving,
Italy has experienced a significant decline in bottom-inequality, reflected in
progressively less negative Z values, at least until the first half of the 2000s,

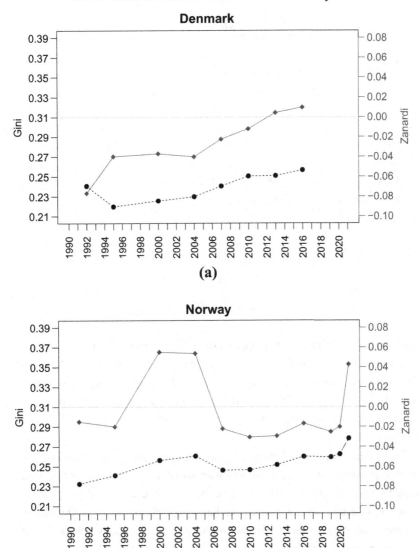

Figure 2.9 Temporal evolution of the Gini (bullets, left scale) and Zanardi (squares, right scale), Northern European countries

Note: The horizontal line represents the zero reference line for the Zanardi index.

before reverting to worsening. Once more, this particular case highlights the limit of the Gini index in accurately capturing inequality. The similar and constant concentration values might erroneously imply a similarity between the two economies, which is not what real data tell us.

The same conclusion applies to the Northern European countries referred to in Figure 2.9, where despite initially displaying relatively low levels of G, there

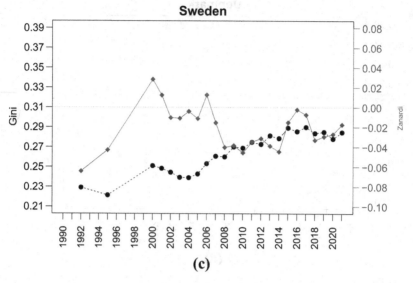

(c)

Figure 2.9 (Cont.)

has been a significant shift in inequality dynamics between the rich and the poor over time. For instance, in countries like Denmark, there has been a transition from highly negative Zanardi index values to values approaching the symmetry line. On the other hand, Norway and Sweden have observed increased bottom-inequality since 2006, with Norway experiencing a notable shift in trend in the last year.

This simple empirical analysis offers a clear demonstration of the importance of incorporating asymmetry into the analysis of inequality. It offers essential insights for a discussion on the accurate interpretation of inequality. In conclusion, these results call for a more detailed approach to understanding income inequality, moving beyond the conventional analysis focused solely on Lorenz curve concentration or entropy indices, in favor of a more detailed analysis that can also emphasize asymmetries in income distributions.

3 The κ-Generalized Distribution

3.1 Introduction

Mathematical statistics is dominated by two large families of distributions. The first is the exponential family, whose main characteristic is that it contains distributions that decay exponentially. Three important members of the exponential family are mentioned below. The first distribution is the generalized gamma distribution, with the probability density function (PDF) $f(x)$ given by $f_Y(x) = Nx^{\alpha\nu-1}\exp\left(-H(x)\right)$, where N is the normalization constant and

$H(x) = \delta x^{\alpha}$, with $\alpha, \delta > 0$, $v > 0$, $x > 0$. A second distribution from the family of exponential distributions is the generalized logistic distribution, which is defined starting from its survival function $S(x) = \lambda/(\lambda - 1 + \exp(H(x)))$, where $\lambda > 0$, which is connected to $f(x)$ by $f(x) = - dS(x)/dx$. The standard logistic distribution corresponds to $\lambda = 2$ and $\alpha = 1$. A third distribution is the Weibull distribution, which corresponds to the case $\lambda = 1$ of the second distribution, and its survival function is given by $S(x) = \exp(-H(x))$.

Besides the exponential family, a second family is that of distributions whose tails are described by the Pareto law $f(x) \approx Ax^{-p}$, with $p > 1$. This family of distributions contains three commonly used distributions defined by the survival function as follows: the first is the log-logistic distribution, with $S = 1/(1 + H)$; the second is the Burr Type XII or Sing-Maddala distribution, with $S = (1 + H)^{-r}$ and $r > 0$; finally, the third distribution is that of Dagum, with $S = 1 - H^r(1 + H)^{-r}$.

In the distributions of the second family, the monomial function $H(x)$ is the same as the one that occurs in the first family. Apart from this common point, there is no other correlation between the two families of distributions. It can also be noted that the three distributions of the second family are the simplest to construct, but there are a variety of other distributions that have asymptotically Pareto tails.

This dichotomy between these two families of statistical distributions leads to some problems on a theoretical level if we keep in mind that there are a large number of systems that are well described by exponential models for low values of the variable x while these models gradually turn into power-law tail models for increasing values of x.

The problem thus arises as to whether the second family of models must be proposed independently of the first family, as has been done in the past, or whether the models of the second family must be replaced by another family which is a deformation of the models of the first family. In the last two decades, this idea has been developed and it has shown that is possible to propose a unique family of models, different from the two above-discussed families. The new family of models, for $x \rightarrow 0$ reduces to the first exponential family, while for $x \rightarrow \infty$ behaves differently to the second family but it also presents Pareto power-law tails. This was possible thanks to the physical mechanism emerging in special relativity which deforms the ordinary exponential function and replaces it with a new function, the so-called κ-exponential function defined as

$$\exp_{\kappa}(x) = \left(\sqrt{1 + \kappa^2 x^2} + \kappa x\right)^{\frac{1}{\kappa}}, \tag{3.1}$$

with $0 < \kappa < 1$ (Kaniadakis, 2001, 2002, 2005). For $x \to 0$ or equivalently for $\kappa \to 0$, the κ-exponential reduces to the Euler ordinary exponential, that is, $\exp_\kappa (x) \approx \exp(x)$, whereas for $x \to \infty$ the κ-exponential reduces to Pareto law, that is, $\exp_\kappa (x) \approx |2\kappa x|^{\pm\frac{1}{\kappa}}$.[9]

The κ-deformed version of the three distributions of the exponential family can be introduced easily as follows (Kaniadakis, 2021):

(i) *κ-deformed generalized gamma distribution*; it is defined through its PDF as

$$f_\kappa (x) = (1 + \kappa v)(2\kappa)^v \frac{\Gamma\left(\frac{1}{2\kappa} + \frac{v}{2}\right)}{\Gamma\left(\frac{1}{2\kappa} - \frac{v}{2}\right)} \frac{\alpha \delta^v}{\Gamma(v)} x^{\alpha v-1} \exp_\kappa (-\delta x^\alpha), \qquad (3.2)$$

with $0 < v < \frac{1}{\kappa}$. In the $\kappa \to 0$ limit, the density function reduces to the ordinary Generalized Gamma density $f(x) = \frac{|\alpha|\delta^v}{\Gamma(v)} x^{\alpha v-1} \exp(-\delta x^\alpha)$. Asymptotically for $x \to \infty$, the density function behaves according to $f_\kappa (x) \propto x^{\alpha v-1-\frac{\alpha}{\kappa}}$.

(ii) *κ-deformed generalized logistic distribution*; the survival function of the distribution is given by

$$S_\kappa (x) = \frac{\lambda}{\lambda - 1 + \exp_\kappa (\delta x^\alpha)}, \qquad (3.3)$$

with $\lambda > 0$. In the $\kappa \to 0$ limit, the function (3.3) reduces to ordinary generalized logistic survival function $S_\kappa (x) = \lambda/(\lambda - 1 + \exp(\delta x^\alpha))$, while for $x \to \infty$ it behaves according to $S_\kappa (x) \propto x^{-\frac{\alpha}{\kappa}}$.

---

[9] It is important to point out once again that the function $\exp_\kappa (x)$ arises naturally within the theory of special relativity. The recently published review paper by Kaniadakis (2024) on κ-statistical mechanics focuses on its foundations and collects the most important applications appeared in the literature in this field in recent years. The self-duality property of the κ-exponential, that is, $\exp_\kappa (-x) \exp_\kappa (x) = 1$, which is identical to that of the ordinary exponential, makes $\exp_\kappa (-x)$ a special deformation of the ordinary exponential. By sacrificing the self-duality property, it is possible to define other deformations of the exponential function. The best known in the literature is that of $\exp_q (-x)$ that leads to the non-extensive statistical mechanics that has found important applications in econophysics (e.g. Ribeiro, 2020, and references within). Recall that given two arbitrary functions $f(-x)$ and $g(-x)$, it is always possible to correlate them so that $f(-x) = g(T(-x))$. If the transformation $T(-x)$ is particularly simple, one can imagine a possible relationship between the theoretical models based on the functions $f(-x)$ and $g(-x)$. The transformation $T(-x)$ that connects the functions $\exp_\kappa (-x)$ and $\exp_q (-x)$ is already known (Kaniadakis, 2001) and has no physical relevance. Therefore, κ-statistical mechanics, which arises in the framework of special relativity, and q-statistical mechanics, which describes the so-called non-extensive phenomenology, are different theories, even though both predict statistical distributions that tend asymptotically to the Pareto law. Rather, it is very interesting that the transformations $T(-x)$ connecting $\exp_q (-x)$ to the Burr-type XII or Sing-Maddala distribution and to the Dagun distribution are particularly simple, as they are a reparametrization or a power-law transformation. This emphasizes the very close connection between the above statistical distributions, which have been used extensively in econophysics.

(iii) *κ-deformed Weibull distribution*; the special case corresponding to $\lambda = 1$ of the previous distribution is the κ-deformed Weibull distribution with survival or reliability function given by

$$S_\kappa(x) = \exp_\kappa(-\delta x^\alpha). \qquad (3.4)$$

The κ-deformed Weibull distribution is the κ-deformed distribution that undoubtedly has found extensive applications, particularly in economics (Clementi, 2023; Clementi et al., 2008; Clementi & Gallegati, 2016, 2017; Clementi et al., 2007, 2009, 2010, 2012a, 2012b; Clementi et al., 2016; Clementi & Gianmoena, 2017) and in seismology (Hristopulos & Baxevani, 2022; Hristopulos, Petrakis, & Kaniadakis, 2014, 2015). Its cumulative distribution function $F_\kappa = 1 - S_\kappa$ writes as

$$F_\kappa(x) = 1 - \exp_\kappa(-\delta x^\alpha), \qquad (3.5)$$

while the related PDF $f_\kappa(x) = \frac{\mathrm{d}F_\kappa(x)}{\mathrm{d}x}$ becomes

$$f_\kappa(x) = \frac{\alpha\delta x^{\alpha-1}}{\sqrt{1 + \kappa^2\delta^2 x^{2\alpha}}}\exp_\kappa(-\delta x^\alpha). \qquad (3.6)$$

After noticing that

$$f_\kappa(x) = h_\kappa(x)S_\kappa(t), \qquad (3.7)$$

with

$$h_\kappa(x) = \frac{\alpha\delta x^{\alpha-1}}{\sqrt{1 + \kappa^2\delta^2 x^{2\alpha}}}, \qquad (3.8)$$

we deduce that $h_\kappa(x)$ represents the *hazard function* of the model.

The derivation with respect x of the survival function permits to obtain easily its rate equation in the form

$$\frac{\mathrm{d}S_\kappa(x)}{\mathrm{d}x} = -h_\kappa(x)S_\kappa(x). \qquad (3.9)$$

The integration of this first-order linear ordinary differential equation with the initial condition $S_\kappa(0) = 1$ permits to write the survival function in the form

$$S_\kappa(x) = \exp(-H_\kappa(x)), \qquad (3.10)$$

where $H_\kappa(x)$ is the cumulative hazard function, defined by means of the integral

$$H_\kappa(x) = \int_0^x h_\kappa(u)\,\mathrm{d}u. \qquad (3.11)$$

After performing the latter integral, the explicit form of the cumulative hazard function is obtained as

$$H_\kappa(x) = \frac{1}{\kappa}\text{arcsinh}\left(\kappa\delta x^\alpha\right),\tag{3.12}$$

which in the $\kappa \to 0$ limit reduces to the standard Weibull cumulative hazard function $H_0(x) = H(x) = \delta x^\alpha$.

A direct comparison between Equations (3.4) and (3.10), incorporating the expression of the cumulative hazard function as provided in Equation (3.12), yields the already established second representation of the κ-exponential function, namely

$$\exp_\kappa(x) = \exp\left(\frac{1}{\kappa}\text{arcsinh}\left(\kappa x\right)\right),\tag{3.13}$$

so that the κ-Weibull survival function assumes the form

$$S_\kappa(x) = \exp\left(-\frac{1}{\kappa}\text{arcsinh}\left(\kappa\delta x^\alpha\right)\right).\tag{3.14}$$

The remainder of the section is devoted to elucidating the main statistical properties of the κ-deformed Weibull distribution, also known in econophysics literature as the κ-generalized distribution after Clementi et al. (2007). This distribution, employing a marginally distinct parameterization from the κ-deformed Weibull, where $\delta = \beta^{-\alpha}$, offers a cohesive framework for describing real-world data, encompassing the power-law tails observed in empirical distributions of income and wealth.[10]

The κ-generalized distribution has showcased remarkable efficacy and is frequently viewed as a superior alternative to other commonly utilized parametric models. Initially introduced in 2007 and subsequently refined in subsequent years, this model traces its roots back to the realm of κ-generalized statistical mechanics (Kaniadakis, 2001, 2002, 2005, 2009a, 2009b, 2013). It possesses a bulk closely resembling that of the Weibull distribution, with an upper tail that follows a Pareto power law for high levels of income and wealth. This characteristic enables it to offer an intermediate perspective between the two previously mentioned descriptions.

---

[10] Econophysics has significantly contributed to the study of income and wealth distributions by adopting a data-driven approach inspired by statistical physics, diverging from the traditional axiomatic methods of economics. This interdisciplinary effort introduced new models to describe income and wealth distributions. Among these, Chami Figueira, Moura, and Ribeiro (2011) proposed a comprehensive model combining the Gompertz curve and Pareto's law to fit the entire income distribution. The Gompertz curve represents the majority of lower-income individuals, while the Pareto law captures the wealthiest segment, with an exponential approximation for middle incomes. Despite these advances, finding a universally accepted single function remains an open challenge.

3.2 The κ-Generalized Model for Income Distribution

3.2.1 Definitions and Fundamental Properties

A variable X following a κ-generalized distribution, denoted $X \sim$ κ-gen (α, β, κ), is characterized by a PDF given by[11]

$$f(x; \alpha, \beta, \kappa) = \frac{\alpha}{\beta} \left(\frac{x}{\beta} \right)^{\alpha-1} \frac{\exp_\kappa \left[-(x/\beta)^\alpha \right]}{\sqrt{1 + \kappa^2 (x/\beta)^{2\alpha}}}, \quad x > 0, \tag{3.15}$$

where $\alpha, \beta > 0$ and $\kappa \in [0, 1)$. The cumulative distribution function (CDF) of this distribution is formulated as

$$F(x; \alpha, \beta, \kappa) = 1 - \exp_\kappa \left[-(x/\beta)^\alpha \right]. \tag{3.16}$$

Figure 3.1 visually depicts the properties of the κ-generalized PDF and the complementary CDF (a.k.a. the survival function), referred to as $1 - F(x; \alpha, \beta, \kappa)$, under various parameter configurations. In each pair of plots, two parameters remain constant while the third is adjusted to demonstrate its effect on the distribution.

The constant β acts as a scale factor, representing the income dimension. Thus, it incorporates the monetary unit, facilitating adjustments for inflation and allowing for cross-country comparisons of income distributions expressed in different currencies. Increases in β correspond to global rises in individual income and average income levels.

On the other hand, the parameters α and κ are dimensionless and shape the distribution. α primarily affects the region near the distribution's origin, while both α and κ influence the distribution's upper tail. A higher κ leads to a thicker upper tail, while increasing α narrows both tails and concentrates probability mass around the distribution's peak.

As κ approaches 0, the κ-generalized distribution tends towards the Weibull distribution.[12] This convergence is evident from

$$\lim_{\kappa \to 0} f(x; \alpha, \beta, \kappa) = \frac{\alpha}{\beta} \left(\frac{x}{\beta} \right)^{\alpha-1} \exp \left[-(x/\beta)^\alpha \right] \tag{3.17}$$

---

[11] From now on, the subscript κ will be dropped in formulas unless it is essential for clarity. For a comprehensive understanding of the properties of the κ-generalized distribution, readers can refer to Clementi and Gallegati (2016) and the additional sources cited therein. A heuristic derivation of the κ-generalized density, showcasing its natural emergence within the framework of κ-deformed analysis, is presented in Clementi et al. (2016) and Landini (2016).

[12] The Weibull distribution, primarily studied in engineering literature, is known as the stretched exponential distribution in physics when $\alpha < 1$. Although sporadic, there have been instances of its use in economics for modeling income data. Some applications can be found in the works of Atoda, Suruga, and Tachibanaki (1988), Bartels (1977), Bartels and van Metelen (1975), Bordley, McDonald, and Mantrala (1996), Brachmann, Stich, and Trede (1996), Espinguet and Terraza (1983), McDonald (1984), and Tachibanaki, Suruga, and Atoda (1997).

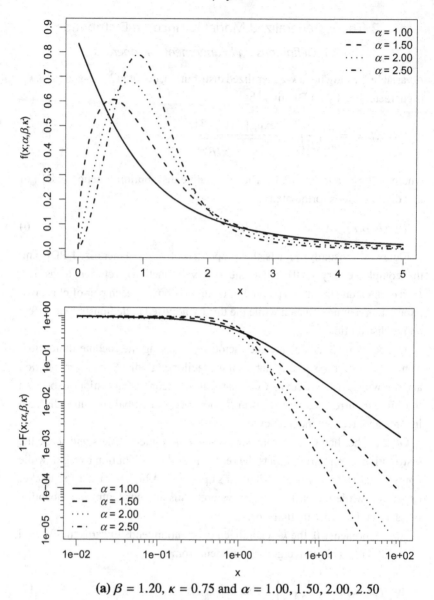

(a) $\beta = 1.20$, $\kappa = 0.75$ and $\alpha = 1.00, 1.50, 2.00, 2.50$

Figure 3.1 κ-generalized PDF (top) and complementary CDF (bottom) across different parameter values

Note: The complementary CDF is plotted on double-log axes to accentuate the right-tail behavior of the distribution.

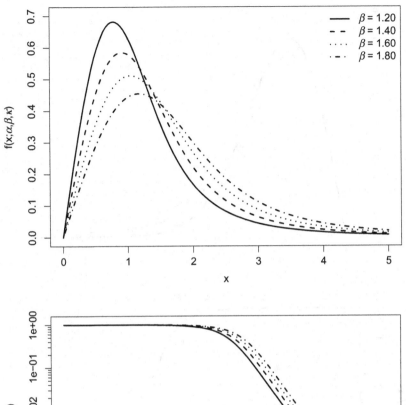

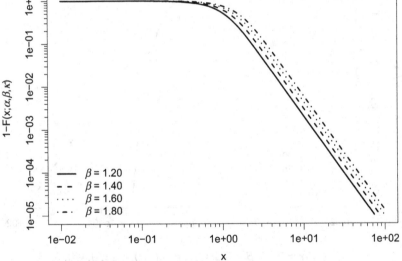

(b) $\alpha = 2.00$, $\kappa = 0.75$ and $\beta = 1.20, 1.40, 1.60, 1.80$

Figure 3.1 (Cont.)

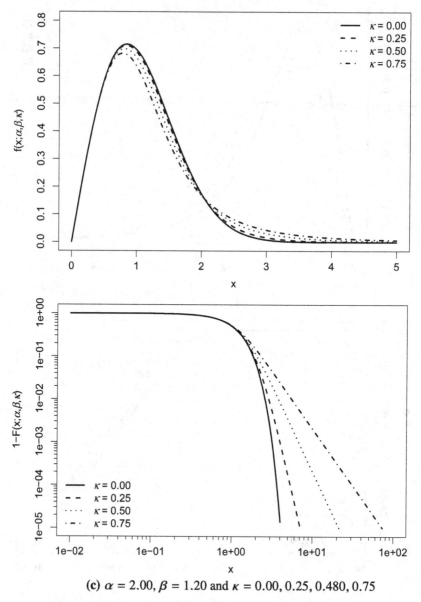

(c) $\alpha = 2.00$, $\beta = 1.20$ and $\kappa = 0.00, 0.25, 0.480, 0.75$

Figure 3.1 (Cont.)

and

$$\lim_{\kappa \to 0} F(x; \alpha, \beta, \kappa) = 1 - \exp\left[-(x/\beta)^\alpha\right].\tag{3.18}$$

As x approaches 0 from the positive side, the distribution behaves like the Weibull model. Conversely, for large x, it tends towards a Pareto distribution of the first kind, characterized by a scale parameter $k = \beta(2\kappa)^{-\frac{1}{\alpha}}$ and a shape parameter $a = \frac{\alpha}{\kappa}$, expressed as

$$f(x; \alpha, \beta, \kappa) \underset{x \to +\infty}{\sim} \frac{ak^a}{x^{a+1}}$$ (3.19)

and

$$F(x; \alpha, \beta, \kappa) \underset{x \to +\infty}{\sim} 1 - \left(\frac{k}{x}\right)^a .$$ (3.20)

Thus, it adheres to the weak Pareto law, as defined by Mandelbrot (1960).[13]

The closed-form expression for the quantile function, derived from Equation (3.16), is

$$F^{-1}(u; \alpha, \beta, \kappa) = \beta \left[\ln_\kappa \left(\frac{1}{1-u}\right)\right]^{\frac{1}{\alpha}}, \quad 0 < u < 1,$$ (3.21)

where $\ln_\kappa(\cdot)$ represents the deformed logarithmic function, defined as the inverse function of (3.1), namely $\ln_\kappa[\exp_\kappa(x)] = \exp_\kappa[\ln_\kappa(x)] = x$. It is expressed as

$$\ln_\kappa(x) = \frac{x^\kappa - x^{-\kappa}}{2\kappa}, \quad x \in \mathbb{R}_+.$$ (3.22)

Thus, random numbers from a κ-generalized distribution can be easily generated using the inversion method.

The median of the distribution is

$$x_{\text{med}} = F^{-1}(0.5; \alpha, \beta, \kappa) = \beta [\ln_\kappa(2)]^{\frac{1}{\alpha}},$$ (3.23)

and the mode occurs at

$$x_{\text{mode}} = \beta \left[\frac{\alpha^2 + 2\kappa^2(\alpha - 1)}{2\kappa^2(\alpha^2 - \kappa^2)}\right]^{\frac{1}{2\alpha}}$$
$$\times \left\{\sqrt{1 + \frac{4\kappa^2(\alpha^2 - \kappa^2)(\alpha - 1)^2}{[\alpha^2 + 2\kappa^2(\alpha - 1)]^2}} - 1\right\}^{\frac{1}{2\alpha}}$$ (3.24)

if $\alpha > 1$; otherwise, the distribution is zero-modal with a pole at the origin.

The rth raw moment of the κ-generalized distribution is given by

$$\langle x^r \rangle = \int_0^\infty x^r f(x; \alpha, \beta, \kappa) \, dx = \beta^r (2\kappa)^{-\frac{r}{\alpha}} \frac{\Gamma\left(1 + \frac{r}{\alpha}\right)}{1 + \frac{r}{\alpha}\kappa} \frac{\Gamma\left(\frac{1}{2\kappa} - \frac{r}{2\alpha}\right)}{\Gamma\left(\frac{1}{2\kappa} + \frac{r}{2\alpha}\right)},$$ (3.25)

---

[13] Alternative formulations of the Pareto law were proposed by Kakwani (1980), expressed as $\lim_{x \to +\infty} \frac{xf(x)}{1-F(x)} = a$, and by Esteban (1986), stated as $\lim_{x \to +\infty}\left[1 + \frac{xf'(x)}{f(x)}\right] = -a$. Given that

$$\lim_{x \to +\infty} \frac{xf(x; \alpha, \beta, \kappa)}{1 - F(x; \alpha, \beta, \kappa)} = \frac{\alpha}{\kappa} = a \quad \text{and} \quad \lim_{x \to +\infty}\left[1 + \frac{xf'(x; \alpha, \beta, \kappa)}{f(x; \alpha, \beta, \kappa)}\right] = -\frac{\alpha}{\kappa} = -a,$$

it follows that the κ-generalized distribution also adheres to these alternate versions of the weak Pareto law.

where $\Gamma(\cdot)$ denotes the gamma function, and it exists for $-\alpha < r < \frac{\alpha}{\kappa}$. Particularly,

$$\langle x \rangle = \beta \, (2\kappa)^{-\frac{1}{\alpha}} \, \frac{\Gamma\left(1 + \frac{1}{\alpha}\right) \Gamma\left(\frac{1}{2\kappa} - \frac{1}{2\alpha}\right)}{1 + \frac{1}{\alpha}\kappa \quad \Gamma\left(\frac{1}{2\kappa} + \frac{1}{2\alpha}\right)} \tag{3.26}$$

represents the mean of the distribution, and

$$\langle x^2 \rangle - \langle x \rangle^2 = \beta^2 \, (2\kappa)^{-\frac{2}{\alpha}} \left\{ \frac{\Gamma\left(1 + \frac{2}{\alpha}\right) \Gamma\left(\frac{1}{2\kappa} - \frac{1}{\alpha}\right)}{1 + 2\frac{\kappa}{\alpha} \quad \Gamma\left(\frac{1}{2\kappa} + \frac{1}{\alpha}\right)} \right.$$

$$\left. - \left[\frac{\Gamma\left(1 + \frac{1}{\alpha}\right) \Gamma\left(\frac{1}{2\kappa} - \frac{1}{2\alpha}\right)}{1 + \frac{\kappa}{\alpha} \quad \Gamma\left(\frac{1}{2\kappa} + \frac{1}{2\alpha}\right)} \right]^2 \right\} \tag{3.27}$$

denotes the variance.

3.2.2 Assessing Income Inequality through the κ-Generalized Distribution

In economics, the notion of inequality traces its roots to Pareto's early investigations (Pareto, 1895, 1896, 1897a, 1897b), which revealed that roughly 80 percent of total income/wealth was held by the top 20 percent. Subsequently, Lorenz (1905) introduced the Lorenz curve, a widely employed method for gauging income/wealth inequality. This curve compares the actual income or wealth distribution with an equal distribution. Under perfect equality, the Lorenz curve aligns with the diagonal of a unit square. Any deviation from this diagonal signifies a more unequal distribution.

The Lorenz curve for a positive and transferable random variable X with a CDF $F(x)$ and a finite mean $\langle x \rangle = \int x \, dF(x)$ is defined as presented by Gastwirth (1971)

$$L(u) = \frac{1}{\langle x \rangle} \int_0^u F^{-1}(t) \, dt, \quad u \in [0, 1]. \tag{3.28}$$

By employing the closed-form expression of the quantile function $F^{-1}(u)$ of the κ-generalized distribution, the Lorenz curve can be represented as indicated by Okamoto (2013)

$$L(u) = I_x\left(1 + \frac{1}{\alpha}, \frac{1}{2\kappa} - \frac{1}{2\alpha}\right), \quad x = 1 - (1 - u)^{2\kappa}, \tag{3.29}$$

where $I_x(\cdot, \cdot)$ denotes the regularized incomplete beta function, defined in terms of the incomplete beta function and the complete beta function, as

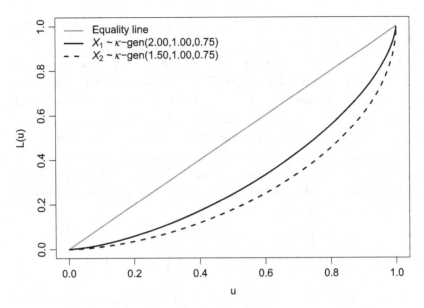

Figure 3.2 Lorenz curves for two κ-generalized distributions

$I_x(\cdot,\cdot) = \frac{B_x(\cdot,\cdot)}{B(\cdot,\cdot)}$. The curve exists if and only if $\frac{\alpha}{\kappa} > 1$. Specifically, if $X_i \sim$ κ-gen $(\alpha_i, \beta_i, \kappa_i)$ for $i = 1, 2$, the conditions for the Lorenz curves of X_1 and X_2 not to intersect are elaborated in Clementi et al. (2010) as

$$\alpha_1 \geq \alpha_2 \quad \text{and} \quad \frac{\alpha_1}{\kappa_1} \geq \frac{\alpha_2}{\kappa_2}. \tag{3.30}$$

The Lorenz curves of two κ-generalized distributions X_1 and X_2 with parameters chosen according to (3.30) are illustrated in Figure 3.2. The depicted curves indicate that X_1 exhibits less inequality than X_2, as the Lorenz curve of X_1 neither intersects nor falls below that of X_2.

Economists have employed different statistical metrics to measure income and wealth inequality. Among these, the coefficient introduced by Gini (1914) is prominent. Starting from the general definition provided by Arnold and Laguna (1977), the Gini coefficient associated with the κ-generalized distribution is derived as

$$G = 1 - \frac{2\alpha + 2\kappa}{2\alpha + \kappa} \frac{\Gamma\left(\frac{1}{\kappa} - \frac{1}{2\alpha}\right) \Gamma\left(\frac{1}{2\kappa} + \frac{1}{2\alpha}\right)}{\Gamma\left(\frac{1}{\kappa} + \frac{1}{2\alpha}\right) \Gamma\left(\frac{1}{2\kappa} - \frac{1}{2\alpha}\right)}. \tag{3.31}$$

Employing the Stirling approximation for the gamma function and taking the limit as $\kappa \to 0$ in Equation (3.31), and after simplification, we obtain $G = 1 - 2^{-\frac{1}{\alpha}}$, representing the explicit form of the Gini coefficient for the Weibull distribution. Additionally, for $\kappa \to 0$ and $\alpha = 1$, the exponential distribution emerges as a special limiting case of the κ-generalized distribution with a Gini coefficient of one half (Drăgulescu & Yakovenko, 2001).

Although the Gini coefficient is widely used, it assumes specific patterns of income disparities across different distribution segments. It is most sensitive to transfers around the middle of the distribution and less responsive to changes among the extremely wealthy or impoverished (Allison, 1978). In contrast, the generalized entropy class of inequality measures (Cowell, 1980a, 1980b; Cowell & Kuga, 1981a, 1981b; Shorrocks, 1980) offers a range of indices sensitive to inequality across various distribution segments. The formula for this class of inequality indices in terms of the κ-generalized parameters is provided by (Clementi et al., 2009)

$$GE(\theta) = \frac{1}{\theta^2 - \theta} \left\{ \left(\frac{\beta}{m} \right)^\theta \left[(2\kappa)^{-\frac{\theta}{\alpha}} \frac{\Gamma\left(\frac{1}{2\kappa} - \frac{\theta}{2\alpha} \right)}{1 + \frac{\theta}{\alpha}\kappa \, \Gamma\left(\frac{1}{2\kappa} + \frac{\theta}{2\alpha} \right)} \Gamma\left(1 + \frac{\theta}{\alpha} \right) \right] - 1 \right\}, \qquad (3.32)$$

where $\theta \neq 0, 1$ and $m = \langle x \rangle$ denotes the mean of the distribution. This class allows different forms of inequality measures depending on the value assigned to θ, indicating the index's sensitivity to income differences across various distribution segments – a more positive or negative θ corresponds to greater sensitivity of $GE(\theta)$ to income differences at the top or bottom of the distribution. Notable limiting cases, derived when θ is set to 0 and 1, are the MLD index

$$MLD = \lim_{\theta \to 0} GE(\theta) = \frac{1}{\alpha} \left[\gamma + \psi\left(\frac{1}{2\kappa} \right) + \ln(2\kappa) - \alpha \ln\left(\frac{\beta}{m} \right) + \kappa \right], \qquad (3.33)$$

where $\gamma = -\psi(1)$ is the Euler-Mascheroni constant and $\psi(z) = \Gamma'(z) / \Gamma(z)$ is the digamma function, and the Theil (1967) index:

$$T = \lim_{\theta \to 1} GE(\theta) = \frac{1}{\alpha} \left[\psi\left(1 + \frac{1}{\alpha} \right) - \frac{1}{2}\psi\left(\frac{1}{2\kappa} - \frac{1}{2\alpha} \right) - \frac{1}{2}\psi\left(\frac{1}{2\kappa} + \frac{1}{2\alpha} \right) \right.$$
$$\left. - \ln(2\kappa) + \alpha \ln\left(\frac{\beta}{m} \right) - \frac{\alpha\kappa}{\alpha + \kappa} \right], \qquad (3.34)$$

where the former is more sensitive to changes in the middle of the distribution, while the latter is more responsive to variations in the upper tail (Jenkins, 2009; Sarabia, Jordá, & Remuzgo, 2017).[14]

---

[14] Equation (3.32) encounters limitations when $\theta = 0$ and $\theta = 1$ due to the expression $(\theta^2 - \theta)$ becoming zero in both cases. To address this issue, we resort to l'Hôpital's rule, which facilitates the evaluation of limits of indeterminate forms through derivatives. Expressions for these specific values of θ are thus derived using this rule. For any $GE(\theta)$ index other than the cases $\theta = 0, 1$, straightforward derivation through substitution is feasible. For further elucidation on this matter, refer to, for instance, Clementi and Gallegati (2016).

Lastly, the inequality measures family introduced by Atkinson (1970) can be derived from (3.32) using the relationship (Cowell, 2011; Jenkins, 2009)

$$A(\epsilon) = 1 - [\epsilon(\epsilon - 1)GE(1 - \epsilon) + 1]^{\frac{1}{1-\epsilon}}, \quad \epsilon > 0, \quad \epsilon \neq 1, \tag{3.35}$$

where $\epsilon = 1 - \theta$ represents the inequality aversion parameter. As ϵ increases, $A(\epsilon)$ becomes more sensitive to changes in lower incomes and less responsive to alterations in top incomes (Allison, 1978). The limiting expression of (3.35) is $A(1) = 1 - \exp(-MLD)$.[15]

3.2.3 Estimation

The estimation of parameters in the κ-generalized distribution can be achieved through maximum likelihood estimation, providing estimators known for their advantageous statistical properties (Ghosh, 1994; Rao, 1973). For a set of independent sample observations $\mathbf{x} = \{x_1,\ldots,x_n,\}$, the likelihood function is expressed as

$$L(\mathbf{x};\theta) = \prod_{i=1}^{n} f(x_i;\theta)^{w_i} = \prod_{i=1}^{n} \left\{ \frac{\alpha}{\beta}\left(\frac{x_i}{\beta}\right)^{\alpha-1} \frac{\exp_\kappa[-(x_i/\beta)^\alpha]}{\sqrt{1+\kappa^2(x_i/\beta)^{2\alpha}}} \right\}^{w_i}, \tag{3.36}$$

where $f(x_i;\theta)$ represents the PDF, $\theta = \{\alpha,\beta,\kappa\}$ denotes the vector of unknown parameters, w_i is the weight assigned to the ith observation, and n is the sample size. This formulation leads to determining the partial derivatives with respect to α, β, and κ for the log-likelihood function

$$l(\mathbf{x};\theta) = \ln[L(\mathbf{x};\theta)] = \sum_{i=1}^{n} w_i \ln[f(x_i;\theta)], \tag{3.37}$$

which translates into solving the following system of equations

$$\sum_{i=1}^{n} w_i \frac{\partial}{\partial\alpha} \ln[f(x_i;\theta)] = 0, \tag{3.38}$$

$$\sum_{i=1}^{n} w_i \frac{\partial}{\partial\beta} \ln[f(x_i;\theta)] = 0, \tag{3.39}$$

$$\sum_{i=1}^{n} w_i \frac{\partial}{\partial\kappa} \ln[f(x_i;\theta)] = 0. \tag{3.40}$$

---

[15] All the measures discussed here depend on distributional moments, the existence of which relies on conditions ensuring the convergence of relevant integrals. Specifically, the Gini coefficient (3.31) is valid if and only if the distribution's mean $\langle x \rangle = \int_0^\infty xf(x;\alpha,\beta,\kappa)\,dx$ converges, a requirement fulfilled only when $\frac{\alpha}{\kappa} > 1$. As noted by Kleiber (1997), parametric income distribution models face similar challenges of existence as those encountered by popular inequality measures.

However, obtaining explicit expressions for the maximum likelihood estimators of the three κ-generalized parameters poses a challenge due to the absence of feasible analytical solutions. Therefore, resorting to numerical optimization algorithms becomes imperative to tackle the maximum likelihood estimation problem.

3.2.4 Utilizations of κ-Generalized Models in Analyzing Income and Wealth Data

Over the past two decades, the κ-generalized model has found extensive application in analyzing income and wealth data across various real-world contexts.

The initial investigation, led by Clementi et al. (2007), scrutinized household incomes in Germany, Italy, and the United Kingdom during 2001–2002. Their study revealed a notable agreement between the model and empirical distributions across all income tiers, particularly within the intermediate range where deviations were noted when using the Weibull model and pure Pareto law for interpolation.

Subsequent studies extended the application of the κ-generalized distribution to Australian household incomes in 2002–2003 (Clementi et al., 2008) and US family incomes in 2003 (Clementi et al., 2008, 2009). In both instances, the model provided a comprehensive depiction of the income spectrum and yielded accurate estimations of inequality measures, such as the Lorenz curve and Gini coefficient.

Comparative analyses, pivotal for assessing relative performance, were also undertaken. For example, Clementi et al. (2010) examined household income distributions in Italy spanning from 1989 to 2006. Their results showcased the superior performance of the κ-generalized model over three-parameter competitors, such as the Singh–Maddala and Dagum type I distributions, except for the GB2 distribution, which features an additional parameter. Similar evaluations were conducted for household income datasets from Greece, Germany, the United Kingdom, and the United States, demonstrating the superiority of the κ-generalized model, particularly in modeling the right tail of the data (Clementi, 2023; Clementi et al., 2012a). Additionally, Clementi and Gallegati (2016) concluded that the κ-generalized distribution offered a superior fit to the data and more precise estimates of income inequality compared to alternatives, leveraging household income data from 45 countries extracted from the LIS Database.

The application of the κ-generalized distribution extends to examining peculiarities within survey data on net wealth, defined as gross wealth minus total debt (Clementi & Gallegati, 2016; Clementi et al., 2012b). These datasets often feature significant occurrences of households or individuals with either null or negative wealth. The model for wealth distribution, based on the κ-generalized distribution, comprises a mixture of an atomic and two continuous distributions. The atomic distribution caters to economic units with zero net worth, while negative net worth data are described by a Weibull function. Conversely, positive net worth values are characterized by the κ-generalized model outlined in Equation (3.15). Analyzing US net worth data from 1984 to 2011 (Clementi et al., 2012b), the κ-generalized mixture model for wealth distribution demonstrated remarkable accuracy, surpassing finite mixture models based on the Singh–Maddala and Dagum type I distributions for positive net worth values. A similar examination carried out by Clementi and Gallegati (2016) explored net wealth data from nine distinct countries.

4 Modeling Income Data Using the κ-Generalized Distribution

In the following, we explore the ability of the κ-generalized model in describing real-world income distributions. Initially, we present the outcomes of fitting the κ-generalized distribution to LIS income data, demonstrating its accuracy in representing real-world data. Subsequently, we assess the performance of the κ-generalized distribution against alternative parametric models proposed in the literature for income distribution. These models are applied to all available national datasets within the income micro-database currently utilized. As previously noted in Section 2.4 of this Element, the statistical analyses presented here are based on LIS microdata updated in March 2024, incorporating additional datasets into the database and thereby broadening the scope of distributions that can be analyzed.

4.1 Results of Fitting to Empirical Distributions

Figures 4.1–4.4 illustrate the outcomes of fitting the κ-generalized model to empirical income data, reflecting the household income distribution in key countries categorized into the four groups discussed in Section 2.4.1: the United States, emblematic of the Anglo-Saxon countries group; Germany, representing the Western European countries group; Italy, representing the Southern European countries group; and Sweden, representing the Northern European countries group. These four cases correspond to the latest available data years for the respective countries within the LIS Database, specifically 2022 for the United States, 2020 for Germany and Italy, and 2021 for Sweden.

The best-fitting parameter values were determined using maximum likelihood estimation, as discussed in Section 3.2.3. This yielded the parameter

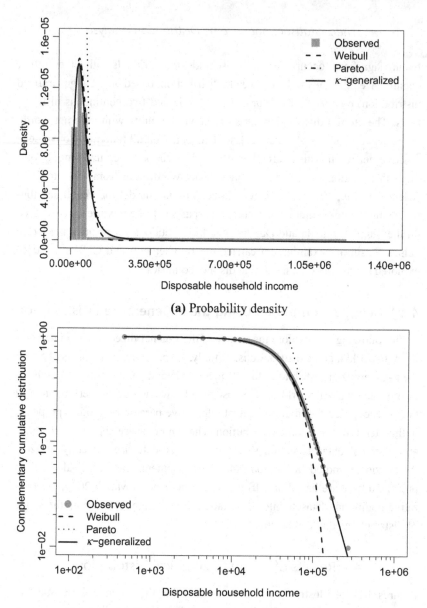

(a) Probability density

(b) Complementary cumulative distribution

Figure 4.1 The κ-generalized distribution fitted to household income data for the United States in 2022

Note: The solid line depicts the κ-generalized model, which fits the data across the entire income spectrum, from low to high incomes, including the middle-income range. This model is contrasted with the Weibull (dashed line) and Pareto power-law (dotted line) distributions. The complementary cumulative distribution is plotted on a double-log scale, emphasizing the distribution's behavior in the right tail. The Lorenz curve plot compares the empirical and theoretical curves, where the solid gray line represents the Lorenz curve of a society with equal income distribution. The Q–Q plot of sample percentiles versus theoretical percentiles of the fitted κ-generalized model shows an excellent fit, with corresponding percentiles closely aligned along the 45-degree line from the origin.

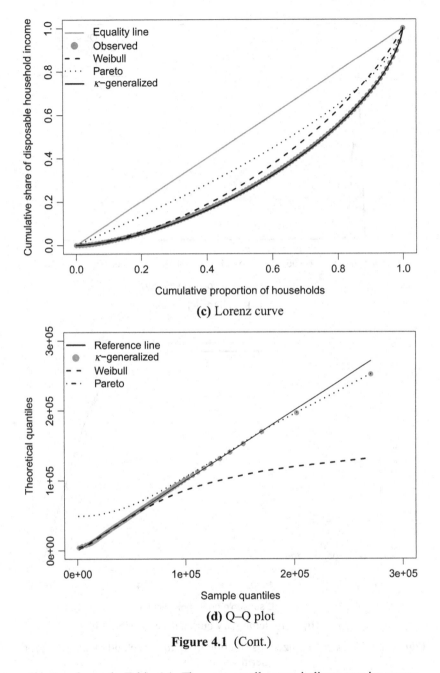

(c) Lorenz curve

(d) Q–Q plot

Figure 4.1 (Cont.)

estimates shown in Table 4.1. The very small errors indicate precise parameter estimation. By comparing the observed and fitted probabilities in panels (a) and (b) of the figures, it becomes apparent that the κ-generalized distribution holds great potential for accurately describing the data across their entire range, from the low-to-medium income region to the high-income Pareto

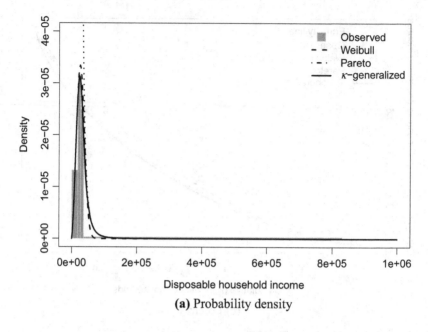

(a) Probability density

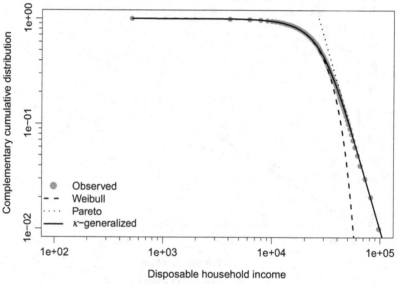

(b) Complementary cumulative distribution

Figure 4.2 The κ-generalized distribution fitted to household income data for Germany in 2020

Note: See note to Figure 4.1.

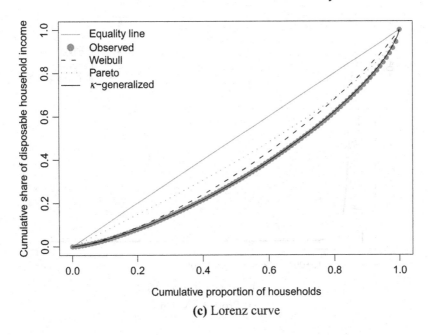

(c) Lorenz curve

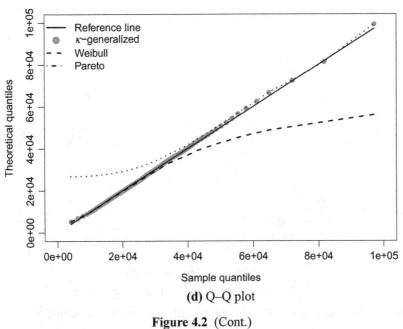

(d) Q–Q plot

Figure 4.2 (Cont.)

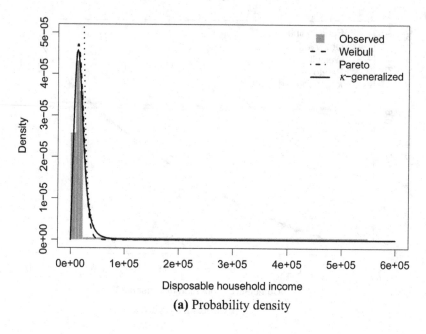

(a) Probability density

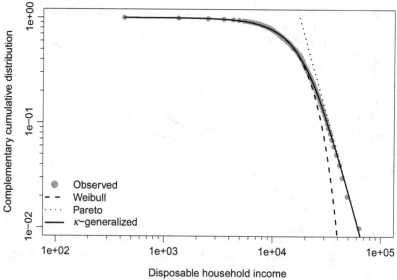

(b) Complementary cumulative distribution

Figure 4.3 The κ-generalized distribution fitted to household income data for Italy in 2020

Note: See note to Figure 4.1.

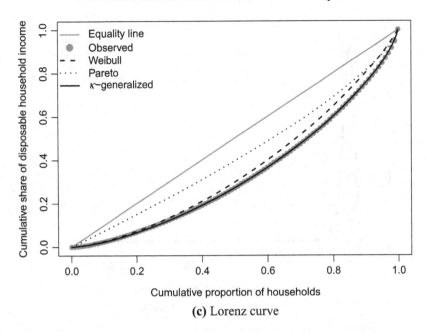

(c) Lorenz curve

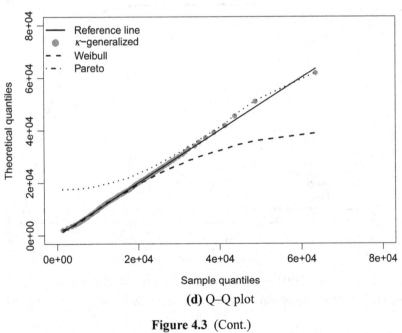

(d) Q–Q plot

Figure 4.3 (Cont.)

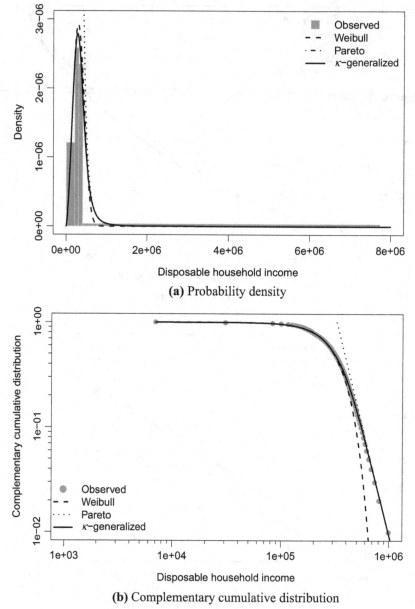

(a) Probability density

(b) Complementary cumulative distribution

Figure 4.4 The κ-generalized distribution fitted to household income data for Sweden in 2021

Note: See note to Figure 4.1.

power-law regime, encompassing the intermediate region where a clear deviation is evident when using two different curves.

Panel (c) of the same figures displays the empirical data points for the Lorenz curve, overlaid with the theoretical curve derived from Equation (3.29)

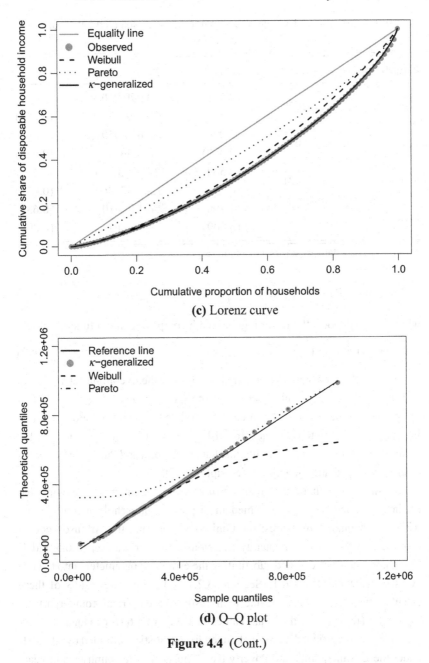

(c) Lorenz curve

(d) Q–Q plot

Figure 4.4 (Cont.)

using the parameter estimates in place of α and κ. This curve is represented by the solid line in the plots and exhibits an exceptional fit to the data. Additionally, the plots juxtapose the empirical Lorenz curve with the theoretical curves associated with the Weibull and Pareto distributions, respectively defined as

Table 4.1 Estimated κ-generalized parameters for selected LIS country datasets

Country	Year	α	β	κ
Germany	2020	2.579 (0.028)	30,999.950 (161.972)	0.735 (0.020)
Italy	2020	2.076 (0.030)	18,634.850 (159.347)	0.569 (0.026)
Sweden	2021	2.564 (0.031)	351,933.240 (2,104.757)	0.619 (0.022)
United States	2022	1.790 (0.009)	56,138.910 (189.766)	0.636 (0.009)

Note: Estimated standard errors in parentheses.

$$\lim_{\kappa \to 0} L(u) = P\left(1 + \frac{1}{\alpha}, -\ln(1 - u)\right),\tag{4.1}$$

where $P(\cdot, \cdot)$ denotes the lower regularized incomplete gamma function, and

$$\lim_{x \to \infty} L(u) = 1 - (1 - u)^{1 - \frac{1}{a}}.\tag{4.2}$$

As evident, these curves capture only a fraction of the overall narrative.

The linear development observed in the quantile–quantile (Q–Q) plot of sample percentiles against the fitted κ-generalized distribution, along with its limiting cases, depicted in panels (d) of Figures 4.1 through 4.4, confirms the validity of the model. It also highlights that the Weibull and Pareto distributions offer only partial and incomplete descriptions of the data.

To indirectly evaluate the precision of parameter estimation, we computed predicted values for mean and median disposable household income, along with two inequality measures: the Gini coefficient and the Atkinson coefficient, where the latter's inequality aversion parameter was set to 0.5 and 1. These computations entailed substituting the estimated parameters into the relevant expressions detailed in Sections 3.2.1 and 3.2.2. The results of these calculations are shown alongside their respective empirical counterparts in Figure 4.5 (for mean and median values) and Figure 4.6 (for inequality measures).[16] The empirical data were obtained from statistics provided by LIS staff under the LIS Inequality and Poverty Key Figures for the countries and years considered.[17]

---

[16] Here, we consider the entire time span for which data for the four countries under consideration are available in the LIS Database.

[17] The full set of LIS Inequality and Poverty Key Figures is accessible in an Excel workbook, which can be downloaded from www.lisdatacenter.org/data-access/key-figures/.

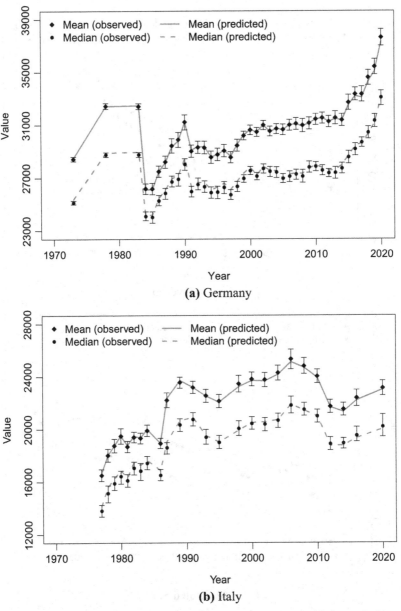

Figure 4.5 Observed mean and median values of disposable household income compared with the predicted values based on the κ-generalized model

Note: To directly compare absolute monetary values across different LIS datasets, mean and median monetary values have been converted into 2017 USD PPPs by dividing them by the corresponding year's LIS PPP, which combines CPI (Consumer Price Index) and PPP (Purchasing Power Parity) deflators to compare real amounts across countries and over time.

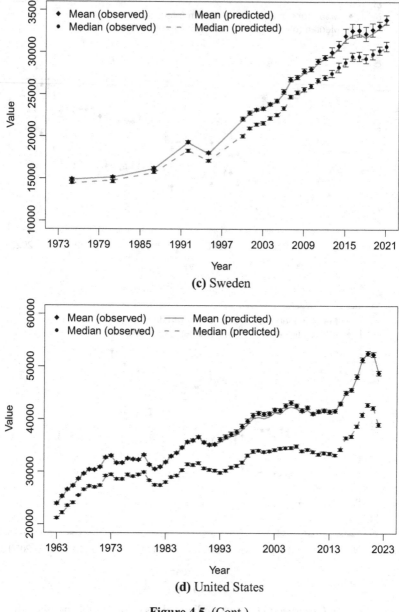

(c) Sweden

(d) United States

Figure 4.5 (Cont.)

As can be observed, the predictions derived from the κ-generalized distribution are largely encompassed by the confidence intervals constructed around the empirical values in the vast majority of cases.[18] This confirms the remarkable

---

[18] In the figures, the vertical bars denote symmetric 95 percent normal-approximation confidence intervals for the empirical values of the statistics, calculated using the bootstrap resampling method with 999 replications.

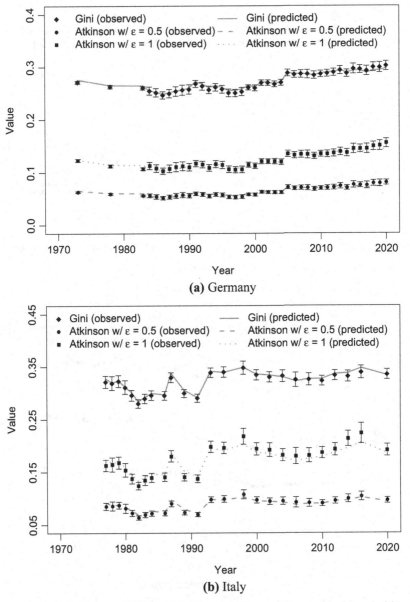

Figure 4.6 Observed Gini and Atkinson indices of disposable household income compared with the predicted values based on the κ-generalized model

agreement between the model and the sample observations. Furthermore, the agreement between the estimates derived from the κ-generalized distribution and the sample values of the considered statistics remains excellent even when considering their temporal trend. Indeed, as shown in Table 4.2, the correlation coefficients between the time series of the considered statistics calculated from the data and those obtained from the estimation of the κ-generalized model are

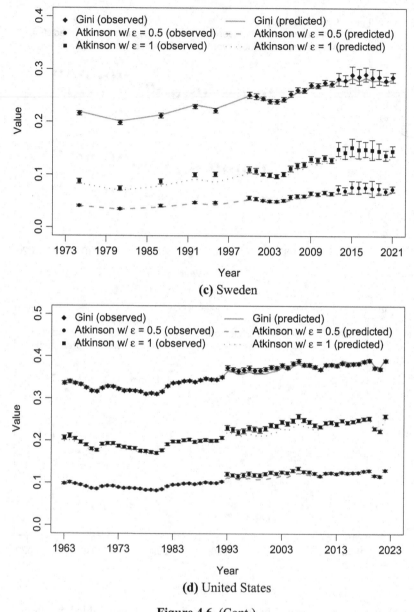

(c) Sweden

(d) United States

Figure 4.6 (Cont.)

close to unity and all highly significant (the corresponding *p*-value is less than 0.001 in all cases).

The good performance of the κ-generalized distribution can also be appreciated by considering its ability to replicate the temporal trend of the Zanardi asymmetry index. As shown in Figure 4.7, the temporal pattern of the predicted Zanardi index values closely mirrors that of the corresponding empirical

Table 4.2 Correlation between selected distributional statistics computed from the data and the corresponding estimates implied by the fitted κ-generalized model

Country	Time span	Statistic				
		Mean	**Median**	**G**	**A(0.5)**	**A(1)**
Germany	1973–2020	0.999	0.997	0.992	0.969	0.974
		(0.000)	(0.000)	(0.000)	(0.000)	(0.000)
Italy	1977–2020	0.999	0.997	0.988	0.973	0.982
		(0.000)	(0.000)	(0.000)	(0.000)	(0.000)
Sweden	1975–2021	1.000	1.000	0.998	0.990	0.988
		(0.000)	(0.000)	(0.000)	(0.000)	(0.000)
United	1963–2022	0.999	0.999	0.985	0.962	0.980
		(0.000)	(0.000)	(0.000)	(0.000)	(0.000)

Note: Values in parentheses denote *p*-values for testing whether the correlation coefficient is statistically significant.

estimates calculated from the sample data and discussed in Section 2.4.1 of this Element.[19] The correlation coefficient values between the empirical Zanardi index and the corresponding estimates from the κ-generalized model, as presented in Table 4.3, corroborate the findings from the visual examination of the figure: all correlation coefficients indeed indicate a strong association between these series, being highly significant with *p*-value lesser than 0.001 in all cases.

4.2 Comparison of Alternative Income Parametric Models

In this section, we present comparisons of the performance between the κ-generalized distribution and other parametric models introduced in existing literature. Specifically, we evaluate the κ-generalized model's ability to approximate empirical income distributions against the three-parameter Singh–Maddala (Singh & Maddala, 1976) and Dagum type I (Dagum, 1977) functional forms. These models are characterized, respectively, by the following probability densities

$$f(x; a, b, q) = \frac{aqx^{a-1}}{b^a [1 + (x/b)^a]^{1+q}}, \quad x > 0, \quad a, b, q > 0, \tag{4.3}$$

---

[19] Figure 4.7, which considers the same countries and time intervals as the analysis presented in Section 2.4.1, does not display the empirical estimates of the Zanardi index to avoid overcrowding the graphs. Zanardi index estimates derived from the κ-generalized distribution were obtained through numerical approximation of areas under the Lorenz curve expressed in the Gini coordinate system (see e.g. Clementi et al., 2019, and references therein).

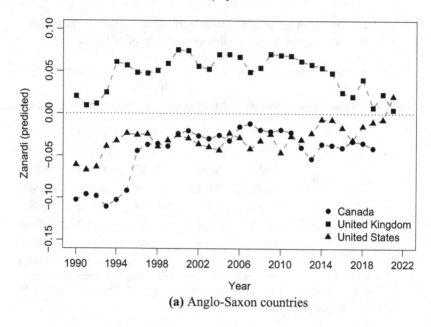

(a) Anglo-Saxon countries

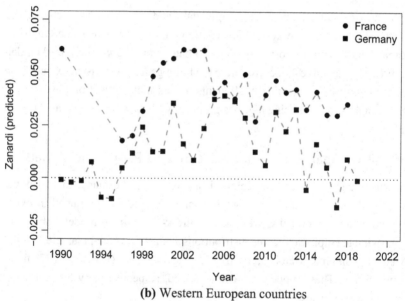

(b) Western European countries

Figure 4.7 The Zanardi asymmetry index based on the κ-generalized model
Note: The horizontal line represents the zero reference line for the Zanardi index.

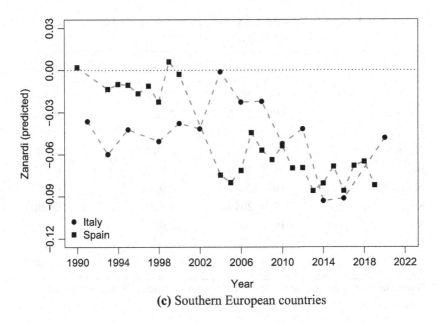

(c) Southern European countries

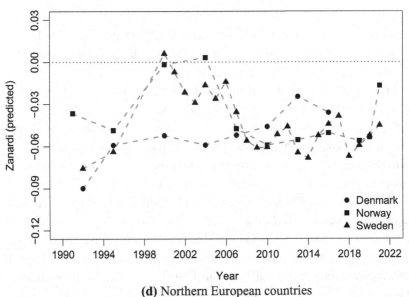

(d) Northern European countries

Figure 4.7 (Cont.)

$$f(x; a, b, p) = \frac{apx^{ap-1}}{b^{ap} \left[1 + (x/b)^a\right]^{p+1}}, \quad x > 0, \quad a, b, p > 0. \tag{4.4}$$

Kleiber and Kotz (2003) offer analytical expressions for distribution functions, moments, and tools for inequality measurement, such as the Lorenz curve and the Gini coefficient. Additionally, Chotikapanich, Griffiths, Hajargasht,

Table 4.3 Correlation between the implied and sample estimates of the
Zanardi asymmetry index

Country	Time span	Correlation	p-value
Canada	1990–2019	0.991	0.000
Denmark	1992–2016	0.967	0.000
France	1990–2018	0.641	0.001
Germany	1990–2019	0.895	0.000
Italy	1991–2020	0.975	0.000
Norway	1991–2021	0.976	0.000
Spain	1990–2019	0.980	0.000
Sweden	1992–2021	0.927	0.000
United Kingdom	1990–2021	0.927	0.000
United States	1990–2021	0.853	0.000

Note: The p-value is for testing whether a correlation coefficient is significantly different from zero.

Karunarathne, and Rao (2018) and Jenkins (2009) provide formulas for generalized entropy measures of the GB2 distribution, from which the Singh–Maddala and Dagum versions can be readily derived.[20]

Our comparisons involve all country datasets included in the LIS Database after the March 2024 update, except for those that are excluded from the calculation of LIS Inequality and Poverty Key Figures. The total number of income distributions considered amounts to 858. For space reasons, maximum likelihood estimates for the parameters of the three models under consideration are not presented here but are available upon request.

Given that a "good" model of income distribution should not only accurately capture the shape of empirical distributions but also closely align with them in a manner consistent with economic welfare considerations, we assess the performance of the three scrutinized models by analyzing the accuracy of selected distributional statistics implied by parameter estimates. These statistics include: the mean; the Gini index, G; the mean logarithmic deviation, MLD; the Theil index, T; the Atkinson index with the inequality aversion parameter set to 1, $A(1)$. For each examined model, the accuracy of predictions regarding these

---

[20] Let X be a random variable following the generalized beta distribution of the second kind (GB2) with parameters a, b, p, and q, denoted as $X \sim GB2(a, b, p, q)$. The Singh–Maddala distribution arises as a special case of the GB2 distribution when $p = 1$, while the Dagum type I distribution emerges when $q = 1$. For further insights into other special cases, refer to Kleiber and Kotz (2003) and McDonald (1984).

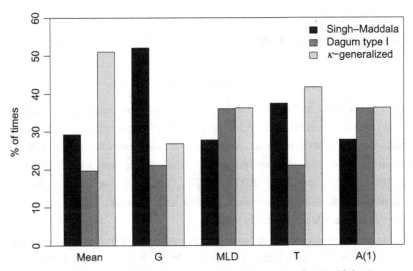

Figure 4.8 Percentage of occurrences in which the Singh–Maddala, Dagum type I and κ-generalized models achieve the lowest absolute percentage error between predicted values for key distributional summary measures and their sample counterparts

statistics is determined by computing the absolute percentage error using the formula

$$APE = \frac{|P - A|}{A} \times 100. \tag{4.5}$$

Here, P represents the predicted values and A represents the actual sample estimates.

The results are summarized in Figure 4.8, which illustrates the percentage of cases where each model achieves the lowest APE for the distributional statistics under consideration. The κ-generalized distribution consistently exhibits a closer match between implied and sample estimates of the mean compared to the Singh–Maddala and Dagum type I models. Conversely, the Gini coefficient estimates are often more accurate for the latter models than for the competing κ-generalized distribution. Therefore, while the estimation procedure of the κ-generalized parameters appears to have generally preserved the mean characteristic across most analyzed country datasets, it has often poorly modeled intra- and/or inter-group variation. However, when examining income disparities across different parts of the income distribution, the κ-generalized model yields relatively more accurate estimates than its competitors for the mean logarithmic deviation, the Theil index, and the Atkinson inequality measure $A(1)$. Given that the MLD index is sensitive to differences in middle incomes, while the T and $A(1)$ indices are more attuned to variations at the upper and lower ends of the income distribution respectively, these findings consistently support the

κ-generalized model's closest approximation to the income distribution shape in a significant number of cases.

5 Conclusion

The κ-generalized distribution model was originally proposed by Kaniadakis (2001) within the context of developing a relativistic interpretation of statistical mechanics for kinetic particles. Since then, it has garnered significant attention in the field of economics, particularly through the works of Clementi et al. (2007, 2008, 2009, 2010, 2012a, 2012b). Notably, in the realm of income and wealth distribution analysis, Clementi and Gallegati (2016) provide a comprehensive reference on this topic.

This probabilistic model defines a new family of distributions characterized by some real parameters θ, indicated by $\mathcal{K}(\theta_K)$. It includes either the exponential family $\mathcal{E}(\theta_E)$ and the power-law family $\mathcal{P}(\theta_P)$. It grasps either *concentration* phenomena about the expected value and *inequality* induced by the tails. This is due to the fact that, beyond *numerical transformations* of data, this model is based on *functional deformations* of the limited and finite support $\mathbb{X} \subset \mathbb{R}$ of a positive and transferable quantity for which the probability field is not *isotropic*. Differently said, for a given positive-transferable quantity $\mathcal{X}$ and a finite sample $\Omega_n = \{\omega\}$ of n observation units, this model well describes the distribution of *masses* $X(\omega) \in \mathbb{X}$ as if their order of magnitude were able to deform the shape of the probability field $\mathbb{I} = [0, 1]$ mainly on the right tail, where few observations far from the expected value weigh more than the majority on the left side fairly below the mean. The κ-generalized manages such quantities that behave *strangely*:[21] that is, cases where below a given threshold $\xi \in \mathbb{X}$ the quantity follows the probabilistic principles of the *exponential family*, i.e., when $X(\omega) \leq \xi$, while beyond it the quantity follows the probabilistic principles of the *power-law family*, that is, when $X(\omega) > \xi$.

The superior capability of the κ-generalized model in describing positive-transferable quantities, which arise from countless repeated interactions among diverse individuals, such as exchanging portions of a given endowment like income or wealth, stems precisely from its *relativistic* nature. This characteristic underscores that the probabilistic principles governing such quantities vary across their spectrum of values. This differentiation, akin to a weak analogy with Einstein's special relativity, underpins the κ-generalized model's ability to shape the probability landscape significantly, particularly impacting concentration and inequality measures.

---

[21] For the mathematics of *strange* quantities, see Landini (2016).

Conceptually, this can be illustrated as follows: within the observation units $\omega \in \Omega_n$, those where $X(\omega) \leq \xi$ exhibit *bosonic* behavior, akin to particles not subject to an *exclusion principle*. Here, many different individuals may possess similar levels of wealth within the range $[0, \xi] \subset \mathbb{X}$, implying $X(\omega) \sim \mathcal{E}(\theta_E)$. Conversely, observations where $X(\omega) > \xi$ display *fermionic* behavior, adhering to an *exclusion principle*. In this regime, only a few individuals may attain similar levels of wealth within the interval $(\xi, +\infty) \subset \mathbb{X}$. Although *bosonic*-like incomes are prevalent while *fermionic*-like ones are rare, the latter typically accumulate the majority of wealth compared to the former.

While it is commonly assumed that the scenario described above is typical, exceptions do exist. Indeed, it is a matter of record that a *fermion*-like recipient such as Elon Musk may possess more wealth than a *boson*-like individual, like many of us, and that there are generally more *bosons* than *fermions*. However, there are instances, be it in certain countries or at different times within the same country, where the rich-*fermions* exhibit greater heterogeneity than the poor-*bosons*, or vice versa.

When the *fermions* demonstrate greater heterogeneity in wealth compared to the poor-*bosons*, concentration on the affluent side of the distribution surpasses that on the impoverished side, denoted as $G^r > G^p$. This situation arises when there are more pathways to wealth than to poverty, characterizing the *top-inequality* scenario identifiable through the Zanardi index of inequality. Specifically, in cases where the asymmetry index of the Lorenz curve is positive, $Z > 0$.

Conversely, in scenarios where the *bosons* are more heterogeneously impoverished than the rich-*fermions* are wealthy, concentration on the impoverished side of the distribution outweighs that on the affluent side, denoted as $G^p > G^r$. This circumstance occurs when there are more avenues to poverty than to wealth, delineating the *bottom-inequality* case discernible through the Zanardi index, which reveals a negative asymmetry, $Z < 0$, of the associated Lorenz curve.

Considering this perspective, the Zanardi asymmetry index of the Lorenz curve emerges as a fitting measure of inequality for several reasons. Firstly, the Z index aligns with the *econophysics* interpretation of the κ-generalized probabilistic model, which capitalizes on the differentiated concentrations of *bosons* and *fermions* to effectively model distributions of positive-transferable quantities such as income and wealth. This alignment underscores its superiority over alternative models in capturing the nuances of wealth distribution.

Secondly, the Z index possesses the capability to identify distributional imbalances across both space and time, a feature unmatched by any other index, including the renowned Gini index, which is confined solely to assessing the overall concentration of the distribution.

Thirdly, the Z index remains robust for space-time comparisons, even in scenarios involving intersecting Lorenz curves. In contrast, traditional measures like the Gini index may yield inaccurate results in such cases, as they disregard the directional aspects of inequality stemming from imbalances in concentration between rich *fermions* and poor *bosons*.

In conclusion, this Element presents two significant analytical findings within the framework of econophysics theory, bolstered by empirical estimates drawn from a comprehensive and up-to-date database encompassing countries worldwide across various time periods.

Firstly, this Element establishes compelling evidence supporting the suitability of the κ-generalized model for fitting distributions of *strange* quantities. These quantities, representing positive-transferable assets, arise from the intricate interactions among heterogeneous agents within a complex economic system, exchanging portions of their endowments. Through empirical analysis, it becomes evident that the κ-generalized effectively captures the dynamics of such distributions, offering a robust framework for understanding the underlying mechanisms.

Secondly, this Element provides clear insights into the Zanardi asymmetry index of the Lorenz curve, demonstrating its efficacy as the most appropriate measure of inequality for *strange* quantities such as income and wealth. By offering a comprehensive interpretation, it underscores the importance of this index in accurately quantifying and assessing the disparities within these economic quantities.

In summary, these findings not only contribute to advancing our understanding of economic systems from a physics-inspired perspective but also offer practical insights into effectively modeling and measuring the distribution and inequality of vital economic resources.

References

Allison, P. D. (1978). Measures of inequality. *American Sociological Review*, *43*, 865–880.

Arnold, B. C., & Laguna, L. (1977). *On Generalized Pareto Distributions with Applications to Income Data*. Ames: Iowa State University Press.

Atkinson, A. B. (1970). On the measurement of inequality. *Journal of Economic Theory*, *2*, 244–263.

Atkinson, A. B. (2015). *Inequality: What Can Be Done?* Cambridge, MA: Harvard University Press.

Atkinson, A. B., & Piketty, T. (Eds.). (2007). *Top Incomes over the Twentieth Century: A Contrast between European and English-Speaking Countries*. Oxford: Oxford University Press.

Atoda, N., Suruga, T., & Tachibanaki, T. (1988). Statistical inference of functional forms for income distribution. *Economic Studies Quarterly*, *39*, 14–40.

Bartels, C. P. A. (1977). *Economic Aspects of Regional Welfare: Income Distribution and Unemployment*. Leiden: Martinus Nijhoff.

Bartels, C. P. A., & van Metelen, H. (1975). *Alternative Probability Density Functions of Income: A Comparison of the Longnormal-, Gamma- and Weibull-Distribution with Dutch Data* (Research Memorandum No. 29). Amsterdam: Department of Quantitative Studies, Faculty of Economics, Vrije Universiteit.

Bordley, R. F., McDonald, J. B., & Mantrala, A. (1996). Something new, something old: Parametric models for the size distribution of income. *Journal of Income Distribution*, *6*, 91–103.

Brachmann, K., Stich, A., & Trede, M. (1996). Evaluating parametric income distribution models. *Allgemeines Statistisches Archiv*, *80*, 285–298.

Chami Figueira, F., Moura, N. J., & Ribeiro, M. B. (2011). The Gompertz-Pareto income distribution. *Physica A: Statistical Mechanics and Its Applications*, *390*, 689–698.

Chotikapanich, D., Griffiths, W., Hajargasht, G., Karunarathne, W., & Rao, D. (2018). Using the GB2 income distribution. *Econometrics*, *6*, 21.

Clementi, F. (2023). The Kaniadakis distribution for the analysis of income and wealth data. *Entropy*, *25*, 1141.

Clementi, F., Di Matteo, T., Gallegati, M., & Kaniadakis, G. (2008). The κ-generalized distribution: A new descriptive model for the size distribution of incomes. *Physica A: Statistical Mechanics and Its Applications*, *387*, 3201–3208.

Clementi, F., & Gallegati, M. (2016). *The Distribution of Income and Wealth: Parametric Modeling with the κ-Generalized Family*. Cham: Springer International Publishing AG.

Clementi, F., & Gallegati, M. (2017). New economic windows on income and wealth: The κ-generalized family of distributions. *Journal of Social and Economic Statistics, 6*, 1–15.

Clementi, F., Gallegati, M., Gianmoena, L., Landini, S., & Stiglitz, J. E. (2019). Mis-measurement of inequality: A critical reflection and new insights. *Journal of Economic Interaction and Coordination, 14*, 891–921.

Clementi, F., Gallegati, M., & Kaniadakis, G. (2007). κ-generalized statistics in personal income distribution. *The European Physical Journal B, 57*, 187–193.

Clementi, F., Gallegati, M., & Kaniadakis, G. (2009). A κ-generalized statistical mechanics approach to income analysis. *Journal of Statistical Mechanics: Theory and Experiment, 2009*, P02037.

Clementi, F., Gallegati, M., & Kaniadakis, G. (2010). A model of personal income distribution with application to Italian data. *Empirical Economics, 39*, 559–591.

Clementi, F., Gallegati, M., & Kaniadakis, G. (2012a). A new model of income distribution: The κ-generalized distribution. *Journal of Economics, 105*, 63–91.

Clementi, F., Gallegati, M., & Kaniadakis, G. (2012b). A generalized statistical model for the size distribution of wealth. *Journal of Statistical Mechanics: Theory and Experiment, 2012*, P12006.

Clementi, F., Gallegati, M., Kaniadakis, G., & Landini, S. (2016). κ-generalized models of income and wealth distributions: A survey. *The European Physical Journal Special Topics, 225*(10), 1959–1984.

Clementi, F., & Gianmoena, L. (2017). Modeling the joint distribution of income and consumption in Italy. In M. Gallegati, A. Palestrini, & A. Russo (Eds.), *Introduction to Agent-Based Economics* (pp. 191–228). Cambridge, MA: Academic Press.

Cowell, F. A. (1980a). Generalized entropy and the measurement of distributional change. *European Economic Review, 13*, 147–159.

Cowell, F. A. (1980b). On the structure of additive inequality measures. *Review of Economic Studies, 47*, 521–531.

Cowell, F. A. (2011). *Measuring Inequality*. New York: Oxford University Press.

Cowell, F. A., & Kuga, K. (1981a). Additivity and the entropy concept: An axiomatic approach to inequality measurement. *Journal of Economic Theory, 25*, 131–143.

Cowell, F. A., & Kuga, K. (1981b). Inequality measurement: An axiomatic approach. *European Economic Review, 15*, 287–305.

Dagum, C. (1977). A new model of personal income distribution: Specification and estimation. *Economie Appliquée, 30*, 413–436.

Drăgulescu, A., & Yakovenko, V. M. (2001). Evidence for the exponential distribution of income in the USA. *The European Physical Journal B, 20*, 585–589.

Espinguet, P., & Terraza, M. (1983). Essai d'extrapolation des distributions de salaires français. *Economie Appliquée, 36*, 535–561.

Esteban, J. M. (1986). Income-share elasticity and the size distribution of income. *International Economic Review, 27*, 439–444.

Gallegati, M., Landini, S., & Stiglitz, J. E. (2016). *The Inequality Multiplier* (Research Paper No. 16–29). New York: Columbia Business School. (https://ssrn.com/abstract=2766301).

Gastwirth, J. L. (1971). A general definition of the Lorenz curve. *Econometrica, 39*, 1037–1039.

Ghosh, J. K. (1994). *Higher Order Asymptotics*. Hayward, CA: Institute of Mathematical Statistics and American Statistical Association.

Gini, C. (1914). Sulla misura della concentrazione e della variabilità dei caratteri. *Atti del Regio Istituto Veneto di Scienze, Lettere ed Arti, 73*, 1201–1248.

Hristopulos, D. T., & Baxevani, A. (2022). Kaniadakis functions beyond statistical mechanics: Weakest-link scaling, power-law tails, and modified lognormal distribution. *Entropy, 24*, 1362.

Hristopulos, D. T., Petrakis, M. P., & Kaniadakis, G. (2014). Finite-size effects on return interval distributions for weakest-link-scaling systems. *Physical Review E, 89*, 052142.

Hristopulos, D. T., Petrakis, M. P., & Kaniadakis, G. (2015). Weakest-link scaling and extreme events in finite-sized systems. *Entropy, 17*, 1103–1122.

Jenkins, S. P. (2009). Distributionally-sensitive inequality indices and the GB2 income distribution. *Review of Income and Wealth, 55*, 392–398.

Kakwani, N. (1980). *Income Inequality and Poverty: Methods of Estimation and Policy Applications*. New York: Oxford University Press.

Kaniadakis, G. (2001). Non-linear kinetics underlying generalized statistics. *Physica A: Statistical Mechanics and Its Applications, 296*, 405–425.

Kaniadakis, G. (2002). Statistical mechanics in the context of special relativity. *Physical Review E, 66*, 056125.

Kaniadakis, G. (2005). Statistical mechanics in the context of special relativity. II. *Physical Review E, 72*, 036108.

Kaniadakis, G. (2009a). Maximum entropy principle and power-law tailed distributions. *The European Physical Journal B, 70,* 3–13.

Kaniadakis, G. (2009b). Relativistic entropy and related Boltzmann kinetics. *The European Physical Journal A, 40*(3), 275–287.

Kaniadakis, G. (2013). Theoretical foundations and mathematical formalism of the power-law tailed statistical distributions. *Entropy, 15,* 3983–4010.

Kaniadakis, G. (2021). New power-law tailed distributions emerging in κ-statistics. *Europhysics Letters, 133,* 10002.

Kaniadakis, G. (2024). Relativistic roots of κ-entropy. *Entropy, 26,* 406.

Kleiber, C. (1997). The existence of population inequality measures. *Economics Letters, 57,* 39–44.

Kleiber, C., & Kotz, S. (2003). *Statistical Size Distributions in Economics and Actuarial Sciences.* New York: John Wiley & Sons.

Landini, S. (2016). Mathematics of strange quantities: Why are κ-generalized models a good fit to income and wealth distributions? An explanation. In F. Clementi & M. Gallegati, *The Distribution of Income and Wealth: Parametric Modeling with the κ-Generalized Family* (pp. 93–132). Cham: Springer International Publishing AG.

LIS Inequality and Poverty Key Figures. (April 15, 2024). https://www.lisdata center.org/data-access/key-figures/. Luxembourg: LIS.

Lorenz, M. O. (1905). Methods of measuring the concentration of wealth. *Publications of the American Statistical Association, 9,* 209–219.

Luxembourg Income Study (LIS) Database. (Multiple countries; February 2024 – March 2024). https://www.lisdatacenter.org/. Luxembourg: LIS.

Mandelbrot, B. (1960). The Pareto-Lévy law and the distribution of income. *International Economic Review, 1,* 79–106.

McDonald, J. B. (1984). Some generalized functions for the size distribution of income. *Econometrica, 52,* 647–665.

Okamoto, M. (2013). *Extension of the κ-Generalized Distribution: New Four-Parameter Models for the Size Distribution of Income and Consumption* (Working Paper No. 600). Luxembourg: LIS Cross-National Data Center. (www.lisdatacenter.org/wps/liswps/600.pdf).

Pareto, V. (1895). La legge della domanda. *Giornale degli Economisti, 10,* 59–68.

Pareto, V. (1896). La courbe de la répartition de la richesse. (Reprinted in Busino, G. (Ed.). (1965). *Œuvres complètes de Vilfredo Pareto, Tome 3: Écrits sur la courbe de la répartition de la richesse* (pp. 1–15). Geneva: Librairie Droz).

Pareto, V. (1897a). *Cours d'économie politique.* London: Macmillan.

Pareto, V. (1897b). Aggiunta allo studio della curva delle entrate. *Giornale degli Economisti, 14*, 15–26.

Park, J., Kim, Y., & Ju, A.-J. (2021). Measuring income inequality based on unequally distributed income. *Journal of Economic Interaction and Coordination, 16*, 309–322.

Pietra, G. (1915). Delle relazioni tra gli indici di variabilità: Nota I. *Atti del Regio Istituto Veneto di Scienze, Lettere ed Arti, 74*, 775–792.

Piketty, T. (2014). *Capital in the Twenty-First Century*. Cambridge, MA: The Belknap Press of Harvard University Press.

R Core Team. (2024). R: A Language and Environment for Statistical Computing [Computer software manual]. Vienna. (www.R-project.org/).

Rao, C. (1973). *Linear Statistical Inference and Its Applications*. New York: John Wiley & Sons.

Ribeiro, M. B. (2020). *Income Distribution Dynamics of Economic Systems: An Econophysical Approach*. Cambridge: Cambridge University Press.

Ricci, U. (1916). L'indice di variabilità e la curva dei redditi. *Giornale degli Economisti e Rivista di Statistica, 53*, 177–228.

Sarabia, J. M., Jordá, V., & Remuzgo, L. (2017). The Theil indices in parametric families of income distributions – a short review. *Review of Income and Wealth, 63*, 867–880.

Shorrocks, A. F. (1980). The class of additively decomposable inequality measures. *Econometrica, 48*, 613–625.

Singh, S. K., & Maddala, G. S. (1976). A function for size distribution of incomes. *Econometrica, 44*, 963–970.

Stiglitz, J. E. (2012). *The Price of Inequality: How Today's Divided Society Endangers Our Future*. New York: W. W. Norton.

Stiglitz, J. E. (2015). *The Great Divide: Unequal Societies and What We Can Do About Them*. New York: W. W. Norton.

Tachibanaki, T., Suruga, T., & Atoda, N. (1997). Estimations of income distribution parameters for individual observations by maximum likelihood method. *Journal of the Japan Statistical Society, 27*, 191–203.

Tarsitano, A. (1987). Fitting the Lorenz curve. *Statistica, 47*, 437–451.

Tarsitano, A. (1988). Measuring asymmetry of the Lorenz curve. *Ricerche Economiche, 42*, 507–519.

Theil, H. (1967). *Economics and Information Theory*. Amsterdam: North-Holland.

Yakovenko, V. M., & Rosser, J. B. (2009). Colloquium: Statistical mechanics of money, wealth, and income. *Reviews of Modern Physics, 81*, 1703–1725.

Zanardi, G. (1964). Della asimmetria condizionata delle curve di concentrazione. Lo scentramento. *Rivista Italiana di Economia, Demografia e Statistica, 18*, 431–466.

Zanardi, G. (1965). L'asimmetria statistica delle curve di concentrazione. *Ricerche Economiche, 19*, 355–396.

Acknowledgments

The authors gratefully acknowledge Joe Stiglitz for fruitful discussions, comments, and critiques over the last five years of cooperation or so. Opinions and comments do not involve the responsibility of IRES Piemonte.

Cambridge Elements ≡

Econophysics

Series Editors

Rosario Nunzio Mantegna
University of Palermo

Rosario Nunzio Mantegna is Professor of Applied Physics at the University of Palermo and an external faculty member of the Complexity Science Hub in Vienna. He is one of the pioneers of econophysics and economic networks, and he co-authored the first book on the topic ('Introduction to Econophysics', Cambridge, 1999).

Bikas K. Chakrabarti
Saha Institute of Nuclear Physics

Bikas K. Chakrabarti is Emeritus Professor at Saha Institute of Nuclear Physics and visiting Professor of Economics in the Indian Statistical Institute, Kolkata. He has co-authored more than two hundred papers and ten books (including 'Econophysics of Income & Wealth Distributions', Cambridge, 2013). In 1995, he organized a conference in Kolkata, where the term "econophysics" was first coined.

Mauro Gallegati
Polytechnic University of Marche, Ancona

Mauro Gallegati is Professor of Economics at Polytechnic University of Marche, Ancona. He has previously held visiting scholarships at Cambridge, Stanford, MIT, Columbia, the Santa Fe Institute, the Brookings Institution, and ETH Zurich. His research includes business fluctuations, nonlinear dynamics, models of financial fragility, and heterogeneous interacting agents.

Irena Vodenska
Boston University

Irena Vodenska is Professor and Director of Finance Programs at Boston University Metropolitan College. Her research is focused on network theory and complexity science in macroeconomics, particularly the modeling of early warning indicators and systemic risk propagation throughout interconnected financial and economic networks. She is a co-editor of the book 'Econophysics and Sociophysics: Recent Progress and Future Directions' (Springer, 2017).

About the Series

Econophysics is a dynamic research field at the interface of physics and economics, in which analytical and computational techniques from physics are employed to study the properties of complex economic, financial, and social systems. Elements in Econophysics explores recent developments within this multidisciplinary research area and covers key topics including: big data in econophysics, financial networks, income and wealth distributions, market microstructure, stylized agent-based models, and sociophysics.

Cambridge Elements ≡

Econophysics

Elements in the Series

Printed in the United States
by Baker & Taylor Publisher Services